# LAW OF THE LAND

**A Practical Legal Guide for Tourists and Business Travelers**

# Puerto Rico

*By Michael L. Moore Esq.*

# DEDICATION

This book is dedicated to the memory of my late older brother, Kenneth Lee Moore, whose tragic murder at 15 years of age inspired me to write this series of books.

This book is also dedicated to my parents, John Henry Moore, and Edna Mae Moore, whose tremendous parenting skills kept me focused on the important things in life: being reverent, getting educated, and prioritizing family.

Finally, this book is dedicated to my beautiful family, my wife Royellen, my son AJ, and my daughter Karla. They inspire me every single day to be kind, patient, and compassionate.

## IN LOVING MEMORY OF:

Belinda Joyce Moore Moss—my beautiful and wonderful sister, who supported me in every positive thing that I ever attempted to do.

Michael Eugene Baker—my dedicated and loyal friend and brother, who always wanted the very best for me.

Sylvia Joyce Hill—my eldest sister, who had a beautiful spirit and was like a second mother to me.

# LAW of the LAND ®
### PUBLISHING for Tourists & Business Travelers

## Travel smart. Stay legal. Stay safe.®

## From local laws to medical guides we've got you covered world wide
## in one digital platform.

# PREFACE

My introduction to the justice system came when I was only 10 years old. My 15-year-old brother was murdered with a butcher knife by a 19-year-old in a simple argument over a torn shirt. I was devastated by his death and sought retribution for his fate that never came. The woman was initially charged with second degree murder, but after plea negotiations, she was convicted of manslaughter and sentenced to only five years in a youthful offender school and ordered to undergo psychiatric care. That was it. Nothing more. The judicial system had run its course.

My family knew nothing about the justice system, and we did not have the tools to advocate for ourselves. No one provided us with a written source to reference for guidance through this process. There was no easily accessible, easy to understand, definitive source to educate ourselves about the legal system that we suddenly and unexpectedly found ourselves immersed in after being victimized by such a violent criminal act.

As I got older, finished college, law school, and ultimately started practicing law, it became clear to me that most people are not knowledgeable about the law or how the judicial process works. If most people are uninformed here in the United States regarding the law and the legal process, how would they fare when in other countries? I realized that tourists and businesspeople who travel internationally needed access to information on how to navigate the legal system in other countries!

For many years, there has been considerable media attention focused on international travelers experiencing legal difficulties while traveling abroad. Most of these news stories gained attention in the United States and abroad because they involved American citizens facing punishment that was considered "unconventional" and "harsh" by United States' legal standards. I recall a news story in 1994 regarding Michael Fay, a young American male, who had broken the law in Singapore. He was convicted and sentenced to be caned and or whipped publicly. While the United States Government weighed in on the inappropriate and cruel nature of the punishment, the young American was beaten because he had been convicted under Singapore law.

Similarly, in recent years, international news stories have garnered head-lines regarding foreign travelers and their issues with the laws of countries that were not their own. Amanda Knox, an American woman, was accused of murdering her roommate in Italy in 2007 and spent almost four years in an Italian prison before being definitively acquitted by the Supreme Court of Cassatio. Kenneth Bae, an American citizen, was arrested in North Korea in 2012 and was convicted for hostile acts against the communist country. He was sentenced to 15 years hard labor but was released in 2014 after efforts by the U.S. State Department. More recently, United States Basketball Star, Brittany Griner was arrested in February 2022 at a Moscow airport on drug-related charges and detained for nearly 10 months, spending much of that time in prison. Her plight unfolded at the same time Russia invaded Ukraine and further heightened tensions between Russia and the United States, ending only after she was freed in exchange for a notorious Russian arms dealer.

It was in 1994 that another personal tragic event occurred that finally inspired me to write these series of books. A dear friend and also client of mine was brutally murdered while on his second honeymoon in Jamaica. News of his murder shocked me and our local community. The legal hurdles his family had to overcome to see that justice was properly dispensed far away from home, in another country, with an entirely different set of criminal procedural rules and laws, was difficult to navigate.

As I was my friend's attorney at the time of his death, his family asked that I act as their "legal liaison" to the Jamaican Prosecutor's Office and to the Jamaican Police Department. I participated in multiple police interviews with my client's widow because she was the primary witness to his murder. As a former prosecuting attorney, I was also allowed by the Court, as a professional courtesy, to sit at the prosecutor's table to consult with the prosecuting attorney during trial. What I observed about the Jamaican trial process from a front row seat was compelling enough to cause me to seriously consider educating the "world" regarding what to expect and how to act appropriately when faced with legal issues while traveling abroad.

One of the realities in life is that, regardless of what country you are in, it is never a pleasant experience to run afoul of the law and be forced to accept that someone else will be making a decision about your pecuniary, proprietary, or penal interests (your money, your property, or your freedom).

It is important to know what the laws are, how they apply to you, and how to navigate the legal system if you are charged with a crime. It is also very helpful to know what resources are available to you if you are the victim of a criminal act. At the end of the day, an "ounce of prevention is worth a pound of cure," so the more knowledge you have, the more ammunition you possess, and the more likely you will have a positive outcome.

If you are traveling to Puerto Rico, the first thing you should pack is a copy of this book! The helpful information and tips contained in this volume will provide a great starting point for knowing what to do (and not to do!) when you arrive at your destination and will help ensure that you have a wonderful vacation or business trip unmarred by tangles with the law.

# TABLE OF CONTENTS

# INTRODUCTION

# INTRODUCTION

As a practicing attorney for over 34 years, I have encountered numerous clients who travel often, but are unaware of the laws of the land they are traveling to.

Therefore, many years ago, I decided to write a series of books that would explain the laws of specific countries. My focus was to explain the laws that may affect travelers in a straightforward manner, without all of the legal language that is sometimes hard for even seasoned attorneys to understand.

## About This Book

The aim of this book is simple. It provides you, the traveler, with a simple, easy to read book that will provide a basic legal guide that explains the law in the country that you are about to visit. It is not intended to educate you on ALL of the laws in a given country. The goal is to provide you with the details of the most common legal and safety issues faced by tourists and business travelers.

I have also provided context with background information on places not to visit, statistics on the country and prevention measures you should take to safeguard your legal and physical safety. Knowledge is a powerful thing and knowing how to stay out of trouble (or how to get out of it!) is important for everyone who travels.

This *Law of The Land/Puerto Rico* book simply helps you become more informed about your legal rights, responsibilities, and obligations in a wide range of subject areas.

Last, but not least, this book does NOT purport to offer legal advice. It does, however, provide the information you need to stay safe, follow the law and navigate around legal difficulties. However, if you do face legal difficulties, the information in this book will provide you with a starting point for solving the problem and obtaining legal assistance should it be required.

## Hypotheticals Used Throughout This Book

From time to time throughout this book, I will explain the law to readers by using hypothetical scenarios. These hypotheticals will be marked by an icon that will be explained in further detail as you read on.

## How This Book is Organized

CHAPTER 1: **About Puerto Rico.** This chapter will provide you with a brief overview about Puerto Rico and its history. It also addresses Visa requirements, monetary advice, and the best times to visit.

CHAPTER 2: **Customs.** This chapter will provide information on what to expect when entering Puerto Rico. It will also explain what restricted and prohibited items are when entering Puerto Rico along with custom's regulations.

CHAPTER 3: **Crime in Puerto Rico.** This chapter provides an overview of the history of crime in Puerto Rico and steps that Puerto Rican officials have taken to curb the high rate of crime.

CHAPTER 4: **Criminal Law Violations.** This chapter will provide information on drug offenses, penalties, true events and questions and answers.

CHAPTER 5: **Alcohol-Related Offenses.** This chapter will provide key points regarding the sale, consumption, and regulations of alcohol use in Puerto Rico.

CHAPTER 6: **Firearm & Ammunition Offenses.** This chapter will provide key points regarding the possession of firearms and ammunition in Puerto Rico.

CHAPTER 7: **Prostitution.** This chapter provides an overview of the history of prostitution in Puerto Rico, laws and penalties, prostitution practices, sex trafficking, sex tourism, health in Puerto Rico, tips to avoid being hassled, a Law of the Land Hypothetical, and the current situation on prostitution in Puerto Rico.

CHAPTER 8: **LGBTQ.** This chapter will provide information regarding the acceptance of LGBTQ people in Puerto Rico, and the laws surrounding homosexuality.

CHAPTER 9: **Sexually Motivated/Violent Crimes.** This chapter will provide an overview of sexually related crimes in Puerto Rico.

CHAPTER 10: **Arrested in Puerto Rico.** This chapter will provide information on what to do if you are arrested in Puerto Rico.

CHAPTER 11: **Jails vs. Prisons: Conditions & Culture.** This chapter will provide information on the conditions and culture of Puerto Rican Jails and Prisons.

CHAPTER 12: **Helping a Friend or Relative Imprisoned in Puerto Rico.** This chapter will provide information on how you can assist a friend or relative imprisoned in Puerto Rico.

CHAPTER 13: **The Administration of Justice.** This chapter will provide information on Puerto Rico's Legal System.

CHAPTER 14: **Crime Victim Assistance.** This chapter will provide information on crime victim assistance along with providing safety tips.

CHAPTER 15: **Police.** This chapter will provide information on the Puerto Rican Police and how to report a crime.

CHAPTER 16: **How to Get Legal Help in Puerto Rico.** This chapter will provide information regarding how to obtain legal assistance for travelers to Puerto Rico.

CHAPTER 17: **Medical Facilities & Hospitals.** This chapter will provide information about how to obtain medical care while visiting Puerto Rico.

CHAPTER 18: **Driving in Puerto Rico.** This chapter will provide information on driving in Puerto Rico, its traffic rules, and road safety tips.

CHAPTER 19: **Nude Beaches & Clothing-Optional Resorts.** This chapter will provide an overview of nude beaches and clothing-optional resorts in Puerto Rico, and the legality and safety of visiting nude beaches in Puerto Rico.

CHAPTER 20: **Unusual Laws.** This chapter will provide information on some Unusual Laws in Puerto Rico, and penalties and fines.

CHAPTER 21: **Traveling Safely.** This chapter will provide information on women traveling alone, crime prevention for families, safety notes for all travelers, and overall advice.

CHAPTER 22: **Tourist Taxation.** This chapter will provide information on taxes that tourists are required to pay in Puerto Rico.

CHAPTER 23: **Long-Term Stays.** This chapter will provide an overview of the consequences for overstaying your visit to Puerto Rico.

CHAPTER 24: **Civil Litigation.** This chapter will provide information about the civil litigation process in Puerto Rico.

CHAPTER 25: **Other Things to Know.** This chapter will provide information on the harassment of tourists, travel and safety, and other practical tips.

**CHAPTER 26:** **Quick Reference Guide.** This chapter is a quick way to get information. It is a condensed version of the chapters in this book.

**Emergency/Important Contact Numbers in Puerto Rico**

**Useful Spanish Phrases**

**Glossary**

## Icons Used in this Book

What do those pictures throughout the book mean? See below:

 **WARNING:** This icon flags information about things you should **avoid** while visiting Puerto Rico. Heed the advice next to this icon to avoid legal perils.

 **REMEMBER:** This icon flags noteworthy information that you **shouldn't forget.**

 **HELPFUL TIPS:** This icon flags information that will help you when entering Puerto Rico, relates to a legal situation, or refers to resources available while visiting Puerto Rico.

 **TECHNICAL INFORMATION:** This icon flags technical aspects of the law. If you are faced with a legal problem, and you want to learn more about the law involved, this information can be helpful.

 **ADDITIONAL INFORMATION**: This icon points to the location of additional information available on the internet.

 **HYPOTHETICAL**: This icon points to hypothetical scenarios to illustrate possible legal problems and the outcome.

 **QUESTIONS**: This icon points to questions and answers throughout the book.

 **TRUE STORY**: This icon points to true events throughout the book.

## Where to Go From Here

If you have a specific question about the law in Puerto Rico as it relates to a particular area, just turn to the chapter that addresses that issue, or turn to the Quick Reference Guide. You can also read the book from cover to cover to obtain a more comprehensive understanding of Puerto Rican laws and resources available should you find yourself in a legal predicament while visiting.

 **Disclaimer:** While the recommendations in this book primarily address U.S. citizens, the information is relevant and applicable to citizens of any country.

# ABOUT PUERTO RICO

# ABOUT PUERTO RICO

## About Puerto Rican

Puerto Rico is an unincorporated U.S. territory located in the Caribbean, about 1,000 miles southeast of Florida. It lies to the east of the Dominican Republic and west of the U.S. Virgin Islands. The island covers approximately **3,515 square miles** (9,104 km²), making it the third largest in the Greater Antilles, after Cuba and Hispaniola.

As of the 2020 census, Puerto Rico has a population of about **3.3 million people**, though this number has been declining due to migration to the mainland U.S.[1]

Puerto Rico is known for its **natural beauty**, including pristine beaches and lush landscapes of El Yunque National Forest, the only tropical rainforest in the U.S. National Forest System. The island also boasts a **rich cultural heritage**, with Old San Juan serving as a historic center filled with colorful colonial architecture, cobblestone streets, and military forts like El Morro. Puerto Rico is a **hub for music**, especially salsa and reggaeton, and its **cuisine**, including dishes like mofongo and lechón, reflects a blend of indigenous, African, and Spanish influences. The island is also famous for its bioluminescent bays, where microorganisms light up the water at night, creating a stunning visual effect.

---

1    https://www.worldometers.info/world-population/
     puerto-rico-population

Historically, Puerto Rico was inhabited by the **Taíno people** before it was claimed by Christopher Columbus in 1493 during his second voyage to the Americas. It became a Spanish colony, and over the next 400 years, it played a key role as a **Spanish military outpost** in the Caribbean. After the Spanish-American War in 1898, Puerto Rico was **ceded to the United States** under the Treaty of Paris. The island became a U.S. territory and, in 1952, a Commonwealth with a degree of local self-governance. However, Puerto Rico's political status remains a topic of debate, with ongoing discussions about the possibility of statehood, independence, or maintaining its current status.

In recent years, Puerto Rico has faced **economic challenges**, including a massive debt crisis and the devastating impact of Hurricane Maria in 2017, which caused widespread destruction and loss of life. Despite these struggles, Puerto Ricans are U.S. citizens but do not have voting representation in Congress or in presidential elections unless they live in a U.S. state.

## *The Capital*

The capital of Puerto Rico, **San Juan**, is the island's largest city and one of the oldest settlements in the Americas. Founded in **1521** by Spanish explorer **Juan Ponce de León**, San Juan holds deep historical significance as both a strategic military outpost and a cultural hub throughout its centuries of Spanish colonial rule.

San Juan's **Old San Juan**, a **UNESCO World Heritage site**, is famous for its well-preserved colonial architecture. The area is home to iconic landmarks such as the **Castillo San Felipe del Morro** and **Castillo San Cristóbal**, both of which were built by the Spanish to defend against foreign invaders. These forts and the surrounding city streets, lined with colorful buildings, cobblestone streets, and historic churches, make Old San Juan a popular destination for tourists.

The city's history reflects its strategic importance in the Caribbean. During the Spanish colonial era, San Juan served as a **key military and trade center** for Spain. Its location made it an important port for shipments of gold, silver, and other valuables, as well as a major stop on the route to the New World. Over time, San Juan evolved into the cultural, political, and economic heart of Puerto Rico.

Today, San Juan continues to be **Puerto Rico's cultural and economic center**. It is home to the island's government offices, major businesses, and many of its cultural institutions, including museums, theaters, and art galleries. San Juan is also known for its vibrant nightlife, eclectic dining scene, and music, making it a bustling and dynamic city.

## *The People*

The people of Puerto Rico, known as **Puerto Ricans**, have a rich and diverse cultural heritage shaped by a mix of **Indigenous Taíno, Spanish, African**, and other influences. Before Spanish colonization in the 16th century, Puerto Rico was inhabited by the Taíno people, who had a well-developed society. The Spanish brought African slaves and settlers, and over the centuries, these groups merged to form the contemporary Puerto Rican population. As a result, Puerto Ricans have a primarily **mestizo** (**mixed**) heritage, with distinct African, Spanish, and Taíno roots.

Puerto Rican culture is strongly communal, with **family** being at the **center of social life**. Many Puerto Ricans value close family ties, and social gatherings often revolve around food and music. Whether on the island or on the mainland U.S., Puerto Ricans maintain a strong sense of community and resilience, embracing their unique cultural blend and vibrant identity.

## *Language*

In Puerto Rico, the official languages are Spanish and English, with Spanish being the predominant language spoken by the vast majority of the population. **Spanish** is used in **everyday life**, including in government, business, and education, and it reflects the island's rich cultural heritage.

**English** is also an official language and is **taught in schools**, but it is **less commonly spoken in daily interactions**. It is more prevalent in urban areas and among professionals in certain sectors, such as tourism and business.

The linguistic landscape of Puerto Rico showcases a blend of influences, with many Puerto Ricans incorporating elements of both languages into their communication. Code-switching, or alternating between Spanish and English, is common, especially in bilingual communities. This bilingualism is a significant aspect of Puerto Rican identity, illustrating the island's connection to both Latin American and American cultures.

## Religion

As of recent surveys, approximately **70 percent** of Puerto Ricans identify as **Roman Catholic**, making it the largest religion on the island, while about 25 percent are affiliated with various **Protestant denominations**. Other Christian sects, including Jehovah's Witnesses and Mormons, represent around 1.9 percent of the population. The presence of non-Christian religions such as Islam and Judaism is modest, and some Puerto Ricans practice Afro-Caribbean religions such as **Santería**, blending African spiritual traditions with Catholicism.[2]

Religious practice in Puerto Rico is typically characterized by strong family involvement, community gatherings, and an emphasis on faith-based rituals. However, secularism has been on the rise, and the number of people identifying as **non-religious** has also grown, particularly among younger generations.

## Affordability

Puerto Rico is generally considered **an affordable destination**, though costs can vary depending on location, lifestyle, and the type of travel experience you're seeking. For residents, the cost of living in Puerto Rico is lower than in many parts of the mainland U.S., but it can be higher compared to other Caribbean islands. Housing, food, and healthcare tend to be more affordable outside of major tourist areas like San Juan

---

2    https://www.worldatlas.com/articles/the-religious-composition-of-puer-
     to-rico.html

and Condado. However, prices can rise in urban centers or beach areas, where demand for housing and services is higher.

For travelers, Puerto Rico offers a variety of options that can fit different budgets. **Budget travelers** can expect to spend around **US$50 to $100 per day**, staying in hostels or affordable guesthouses and eating at local restaurants or food stalls. Those with a **mid-range budget** will likely spend between **US$100 to $200 per day**, enjoying comfortable accommodations, meals at mid-range restaurants, and participating in tours or activities like hiking or sightseeing. For **luxury travelers**, costs can increase significantly, with upscale resorts, private tours, and fine dining pushing daily expenses above **US$250 per day**.

## Puerto Rico, the Basics

*How to Get There?*

Since Puerto Rico is a U.S. territory, U.S. citizens do not need a passport to visit, and traveling to Puerto Rico is considered domestic travel. International visitors will need a valid passport and may require a visa, depending on their nationality.

Getting to Puerto Rico is fairly straightforward, with several airlines offering direct flights from major cities in the U.S. and other countries. The biggest airports in Puerto Rico are:

1. **Luis Muñoz Marín International Airport (SJU) – San Juan.** This is the largest and busiest airport in Puerto Rico, located about 15 minutes east of San Juan. It handles the majority of both domestic and international flights to and from the island. Many major U.S. airlines and international carriers operate out of SJU.

2. **Rafael Hernández Airport (BQN) – Aguadilla.** Located on the western side of the island, this airport serves more limited international and domestic flights, but it's a good option for those visiting the western regions of Puerto Rico.

3. **Mercedita Airport (PSE) – Ponce.** This is a smaller airport located in the southern part of Puerto Rico. It mostly serves domestic flights and some regional routes, primarily from the U.S. mainland.

Several major airlines provide direct flights to Puerto Rico from the mainland U.S. and abroad. Some of the most prominent carriers include:

- American Airlines
- JetBlue Airways
- Southwest Airlines
- United Airlines
- Delta Air Lines
- Spirit Airlines
- Alaska Airlines

These airlines offer frequent flights to Puerto Rico from major U.S. cities, including **New York, Miami, Orlando, Chicago,** and **Boston.** International flights also arrive from **Europe, Latin America,** and the **Caribbean.**

The **cost of flights** to Puerto Rico varies depending on the time of year, with some periods being significantly cheaper than others. The cheapest time to visit Puerto Rico is typically **during the low season,** which runs from **April to November.** This is when airfares are the most affordable, especially in May, September, and October. These months coincide with the off-peak tourist season, and there's less demand for flights. However, be aware that this period coincides with **hurricane season** (June to November), so there's a higher chance of rain and storms.

The **winter months** (December to March) see the **highest demand** for flights, as Puerto Rico is a popular destination for U.S. citizens seeking a warm escape from the colder weather. Flight prices tend to peak during **Christmas, New Year's,** and **spring break** (March). If you're planning to travel during this period, booking well in advance can help secure better fares.

For the best balance between affordable flights and good weather, the **shoulder seasons** are ideal. **Late November to early December** and **April** typically offer lower fares than peak winter months, while avoiding the wettest months of the year.

*When to Visit?*

The best time to visit Puerto Rico depends on weather, crowds, and activities:

- **Weather:** The **dry season** from **December to April** offers the best weather with sunny days and low humidity, making it perfect for beaches, water activities, and outdoor sightseeing. The **rainy season** (May to November) is more humid with occasional rain and the possibility of hurricanes, though it still offers plenty of sunshine.

- **Crowds: Peak season** is from **December to April**, especially during holidays and spring break, when the island is most crowded and prices are higher. The **off-season** (May to November) sees fewer tourists, lower prices, and less crowded attractions, but there's a higher chance of rain.

- **Festivals & Events:** Puerto Rico hosts vibrant festivals year-round, which tend to draw bigger crowds:

  - **Fiesta de la Calle San Sebastián** (January) in San Juan.
  - **Carnaval de Ponce** (February).
  - **Puerto Rico Heineken JazzFest** (March).
  - **Dia de San Juan** (June).
  - **Christmas celebrations** (December) with parades, music, and traditional food.

 **Do I Need a Visa?**

No. U.S. citizens do not need a visa to travel to Puerto Rico, as it is a U.S. territory. Travel to Puerto Rico is considered domestic travel, so U.S. citizens only need a valid government-issued ID, such as a driver's license or passport for air travel. A passport is not required for U.S. citizens.

For non-U.S. citizens, the visa requirements depend on their nationality. If you're traveling from another country, you will need a valid U.S. visa or an ESTA (Electronic System for Travel Authorization) under the Visa Waiver Program if you're from a participating country. If you're already in the U.S. with legal status, such as on a tourist visa, you can travel to Puerto Rico without needing a separate visa.

*How to Get Around*

In Puerto Rico, getting around is relatively easy, though the most convenient options depend on where you're staying and what you plan to do. While Puerto Rico has public transportation, most tourists find it more practical to use other methods for greater flexibility and convenience.

**Rental Cars** are the most convenient way to explore the island, especially if you want to visit multiple regions or venture into more remote areas. Major car rental agencies are available at the airport and in cities like San Juan. Renting a car gives you the freedom to explore beaches, hiking trails, and off-the-beaten-path locations at your own pace. Keep in mind that parking can be limited and expensive in busy areas like Old San Juan, so be prepared for potential parking fees.

**Ridesharing** services like **Uber** are available in major cities like San Juan, Condado, and Isla Verde. Uber is a popular and affordable way to get around without the need for a rental car. It's especially useful if you're traveling within the city or need a ride to a specific tourist attraction.

**Taxis** are also available, though they tend to be more expensive than ridesharing services.

**Public Buses** are available but limited in their coverage and less reliable for tourists. The **Metrobus** system operates throughout San Juan and nearby areas, and **Públicos** (shared vans) are used for short distances, particularly between towns. While affordable, public buses may not be the best choice for tourists looking to explore the island's attractions.

**Walking** is a great way to get around in pedestrian-friendly areas, especially in cities like **Old San Juan**, where the narrow streets are ideal for exploring on foot. Most of the historic landmarks and attractions in Old San Juan are close together, so walking is often the easiest way to get around.

**Trolleys and Shuttles:** In places like **Old San Juan**, there are free trolley services that operate on specific routes to help tourists get around the historic district. Some resorts or tourist areas also offer shuttles that can transport visitors between popular spots.

 **Monetary Advice**

Puerto Rico uses the **U.S. Dollar** (**USD**) as its official currency, so there is no need to exchange money if you're traveling from the United States. For international visitors, the **exchange rate** will depend on their home currency, but U.S. Dollars are widely accepted, and ATMs that dispense USD are common throughout the island.

Most establishments in Puerto Rico, including hotels, restaurants, and shops, accept major **credit cards** such as **Visa**, **Mastercard**, and **American Express**. You should have no trouble using your credit card for purchases, but it's always a good idea to notify your bank or credit card company of your travel dates to avoid any issues with fraud alerts.

While the U.S. Dollar is the official currency, **foreign currencies** (like the Euro or other international currencies) are **not typically accepted** in Puerto Rico, so it's advisable to exchange any foreign currency into USD before your trip.

**ATMs** are **widely available**, and they usually offer the best exchange rates for withdrawing cash. Just be mindful of any **foreign transaction fees** your bank may charge for ATM withdrawals or credit card payments abroad.

### Bargaining

In Puerto Rico, bargaining is **not common practice** in most situations, especially in larger shops, malls, or chain stores. Prices are generally fixed. However, in markets or with street vendors, you may find opportunities for negotiating prices, especially if you're purchasing souvenirs or small items. In these cases, offering a polite and respectful counteroffer can sometimes lead to a better deal. Keep in mind that bargaining is not expected, and showing respect for local culture and prices is always appreciated.

### Tipping

Tipping in Puerto Rico is **similar to the mainland** U.S. Customs include leaving a tip of **15 to 20 percent** at **restaurants**, unless a service charge is already included. For bartenders, it's typical to tip US$1 to $2 per drink, or around 15 percent of the total bill. **Taxis** and **Uber** drivers generally receive a tip of **10 to 15 percent** of the fare, or you can round up for shorter rides. Hotel staff usually expect **US$1 to $2 per bag** for bellhops and **US$2 to $5 per night** for **housekeeping**. For **tour guides**, a tip of **US$10 to $20 per person** is common, depending on the tour length and service.

## Puerto Rican Hospitality

Puerto Rican hospitality is known for being **warm, friendly,** and **generous**. The island's people are eager to share their culture, and visitors are often greeted with a warm embrace or a kiss on the cheek, even by strangers. Puerto Ricans take pride in offering food and drinks, such as coquito or local dishes like lechón and mofongo, to guests.

Politeness is expressed through friendly greetings like "buenos días" and maintaining eye contact, while being distant or formal can be seen as impolite. Visitors should show respect by engaging in conversation, trying to learn about the culture, and accepting offers of food or drink.

Being mindful of local customs, such as bringing a small gift when visiting someone's home, is appreciated. It's also important to avoid making negative comments about the island or its people, as Puerto Ricans are proud of their heritage.

# CUSTOMS

CHAPTER 2

# CUSTOMS

## Travelers Entering Puerto Rico

To enter Puerto Rico, travelers need to meet a few basic requirements:

1.  **Valid Passport or U.S. ID:** For U.S. citizens, a valid government-issued ID, such as a driver's license or passport, is required. International travelers must have a valid passport to enter Puerto Rico, as it is a U.S. territory.

2.  **Return or Onward Ticket:** While a return or onward ticket isn't always required for U.S. citizens, it may be necessary for international travelers to show proof of their plan to leave Puerto Rico within the allowed time frame (typically 90 days for most tourists).

3.  **Visa (If Applicable):** Travelers from certain countries may require a **U.S. visa** to enter Puerto Rico. Citizens from countries in the **Visa Waiver Program** (such as the U.K., Canada, and most European Union nations) do not need a visa for stays of up to 90 days. Others may need to apply for a visa through a U.S. embassy or consulate.

4.  **Proof of Sufficient Funds:** Occasionally, travelers may need to show proof of sufficient funds to cover their stay, especially when entering Puerto Rico from abroad. This can be in the form of bank statements, credit cards, or other financial documentation.

5. **Vaccination Requirements:** There are currently no mandatory vaccination requirements to enter Puerto Rico, but travelers are encouraged to be up to date on routine vaccinations. If arriving from a country with a yellow fever risk, a yellow fever vaccination certificate may be required.

6. **Health Insurance:** Although not mandatory for entry, having travel health insurance is highly recommended, especially in case of medical emergencies. Some travelers may be asked to show proof of coverage.

Upon arrival in Puerto Rico, the process is straightforward. After disembarking, international travelers will go through **U.S. immigration**, presenting their passport, possibly a return or onward ticket, and any necessary documents like proof of funds or a visa. Once cleared through immigration, travelers will collect their luggage and go through **customs**. Customs checks are relaxed, but travelers should declare any restricted items like fresh produce or meats.

Currency exchange booths and ATMs are available at the airport, though U.S. dollars are the official currency and are widely accepted throughout the island. Transportation options include taxis, ridesharing services like Uber, and car rental agencies. No arrival tax is required, but a departure fee may apply, often included in airfare (tourist taxation is discussed in Chapter 22).

Puerto Rican airports are modern, welcoming, and well-equipped for travelers, with the island's warm hospitality reflected in the atmosphere. Be sure to check for any travel advisories or health requirements before departure. With proper preparation, entering Puerto Rico should be a smooth and hassle-free process.

## Customs Entitlements and Monetary Restrictions[3]

Since Puerto Rico is a U.S. territory, U.S. customs and regulations apply to travelers arriving on the island. As such, Puerto Rico follows the same customs rules as the mainland U.S.

Here are general guidelines on what you can bring into Puerto Rico:

### *Currency Restrictions*

Travelers entering Puerto Rico, like anywhere in the U.S., must declare **currency or monetary instruments** exceeding **US$10,000** to U.S. Customs and Border Protection (CBP). This includes cash, traveler's checks, money orders, negotiable instruments, or any other form of monetary value. If you are carrying **more than US$10,000**, you must **declare it** at customs, even if it's not in U.S. dollars. For amounts **below US$10,000**, you are **not required to declare** anything. However, it is advisable to avoid carrying large sums of cash when traveling. ATMs are available throughout Puerto Rico, and credit cards are widely accepted.

### *Permitted Items*

1. **Personal Belongings:** You are allowed to bring personal items like clothing, toiletries, and electronics for personal use. There are no specific limits on these items as long as they are not for resale.

2. **Alcohol and Tobacco:** U.S. Customs allows **1 liter of alcohol** per person over the age of 21 to be brought into Puerto Rico duty-free. If you exceed this limit, you will be required to pay customs duties. The same applies to **tobacco products**—travelers are allowed **200 cigarettes** or **100 cigars** per person duty-free.

3. **Food:** Most commercially packaged food is allowed, though there are restrictions on items like **fresh produce**, **meat**, and **dairy products.** Any items that could carry pests or diseases, such as fruits,

---

3    https://www.visahq.com/puerto-rico/customs/

vegetables, meats, and plants, must be declared and may be prohibited if they pose a risk to local agriculture or wildlife.

4. **Medicines: Prescription medications** for personal use are generally allowed, but they must be in their original packaging. It's a good idea to carry a copy of your prescription. **Over-the-counter medications** are also allowed but should be in their original packaging and quantities consistent with personal use.

When entering Puerto Rico, you **must declare any items that exceed the personal exemption limits or are subject to duty**. Common items to declare include alcohol, tobacco, food items, or expensive goods like electronics. Generally, U.S. customs officers will ask travelers about their purchases and may inspect luggage for items that need to be declared.

Check U.S. Customs regulations before traveling to ensure that any new or updated restrictions are followed, especially regarding food or agricultural items, as these regulations can change.

 ## Restricted and Prohibited Items

Certain items are prohibited or restricted from being imported into Puerto Rico, which follows the same customs regulations as the U.S. to ensure the protection of local agriculture, safety, and security. It is essential to be aware of these restrictions to avoid penalties or delays at customs.

**Fresh fruits, vegetables, plants, seeds**, and **soil** are **highly regulated**. These items are restricted due to the risk of introducing harmful pests or diseases that could damage local agriculture. It is important to avoid bringing any fresh food, plants, or agricultural products into Puerto Rico unless you have obtained the necessary permits.

The importation of **meats**, **dairy products**, and **certain animal products** is also **strictly controlled**. Bringing these items without proper declaration can result in confiscation. If you plan to carry such items, check with U.S. Customs and Border Protection (CBP) to see if special permits or certifications are required.

Prohibited items include:

- **Illegal drugs and controlled substances:** U.S. law prohibits the possession of illegal drugs, including marijuana, regardless of its legality in other jurisdictions. Violations can lead to severe penalties.
- **Firearms and ammunition:** Importing firearms and ammunition requires specific permits. Without the necessary permits, firearms will be seized, and travelers may face legal action.
- **Items made from endangered species:** Products such as coral, turtle shells, ivory, and other items derived from endangered species are protected under U.S. and international law. These items are illegal to bring into Puerto Rico.
- **Fireworks and explosives:** The importation of fireworks or explosives is prohibited unless you have obtained the appropriate permits from the U.S. government.

Bringing restricted or prohibited items into Puerto Rico can have **serious consequences**. These include confiscation of the items, fines, delays, or further legal actions. In cases of illegal substances, firearms, or endangered species products, travelers may face **criminal charges**, **detention**, or **deportation**. Even if you unknowingly bring in prohibited items like fresh produce, they will likely be seized by customs officials and destroyed.

To avoid complications, always declare any potentially restricted or prohibited items upon arrival and consult with U.S. Customs before your trip to ensure you're fully informed of the regulations.

 For a more detailed list of restricted and prohibited items when traveling to Puerto Rico, visit the U.S. Customs and Border Protection website at **https://www.cbp.gov/**.

## Five Practical Tips to Know Before You Go

1.  **Learn Basic Spanish Phrases:** While English is widely spoken in Puerto Rico, especially in tourist areas, learning a few basic Spanish phrases can enhance your experience. Simple greetings like "*Hola*" (hello), "*Gracias*" (thank you), and "*Por favor*" (please) go a long way in showing respect for local culture, and locals appreciate the effort.

2.  **Pack for Tropical Weather:** Puerto Rico has a tropical climate, so lightweight clothing, comfortable shoes, and sunscreen are essential. If you plan to visit the rainforest or go hiking, pack sturdy footwear, insect repellent, and a light rain jacket. The island can also get cooler in the mountains, so bring a light sweater or jacket just in case.

3.  **Get Travel Insurance:** It's a good idea to have travel insurance when visiting Puerto Rico, especially if you're planning to engage in outdoor activities like hiking, surfing, or zip-lining. While Puerto Rico's medical care is good, travel insurance will cover unexpected medical costs or trip disruptions.

4.  **Know Your Transportation Options:** Puerto Rico's public transportation can be limited outside major cities. Renting a car is recommended if you plan on exploring beyond San Juan or other tourist hubs. Taxis, rideshare services like Uber, and local buses are also options, but they might not always be as convenient or readily available in remote areas.

5.  **Check Entry Requirements:** U.S. citizens don't need a passport to visit Puerto Rico, but make sure your government-issued ID (such as a driver's license) is valid. International visitors will need a valid passport to enter. Also, while Puerto Rico is a U.S. territory, always verify the latest travel regulations, such as any health-related entry requirements, before your trip.

# CRIME IN PUERTO RICO

IN THIS CHAPTER

- Overview
- Crime Hotspots in Puerto Rico
- Crime Statistics
- Quick Safety Tips

# CRIME IN PUERTO RICO

## Overview

Puerto Rico is **generally safe** for tourists, especially in popular areas like Old San Juan, Condado, Isla Verde, and Rincón. While millions of visitors enjoy the island's beaches and resorts without incident, some neighborhoods, particularly in San Juan and rural areas, have higher crime rates. **Petty crimes** such as **pickpocketing** and **scams** can occur in crowded tourist spots, especially at night. Violent crime is less common in tourist areas but has been reported in certain regions.

The island faces **challenges with crime**, particularly **in urban centers**, often linked to issues like **poverty, drug trafficking**, and **gang violence**. Despite fluctuations in the overall crime rate, law enforcement efforts and community programs have made some progress in reducing crime in specific areas. **Visitors should remain cautious, especially in less populated regions, and stay aware of their surroundings.**

## Crime Hotspots in Puerto Rico[4]

Puerto Rico presents a complex crime landscape that can vary significantly between regions. While Puerto Rico is a popular tourist destination and most areas are safe, there are certain neighborhoods and

---

4    https://crimegrade.org/safest-places-in-puerto-rico/

regions with higher crime rates. The **crime hotspots** tend to be in more **urban or impoverished areas**, often linked to issues such as drug trafficking and gang violence.

**San Juan**, Puerto Rico's capital and largest city, has both high-crime and low-crime areas. While districts like **Old San Juan, Condado,** and **Isla Verde** are popular with tourists and relatively safe, areas such as **Santurce, La Perla,** and **Rio Piedras** have a higher incidence of crime, including violent offenses like robberies and assaults. **Santurce**, in particular, has been known for gang-related activity and occasional drug-related violence.

**Bayamón** is one of Puerto Rico's largest cities and has had ongoing issues with violent crime. It is not a typical tourist destination, but travelers visiting surrounding areas or passing through should be cautious, especially in lower-income neighborhoods.

**Ponce**, the second-largest city on the island, located on the southern coast, has seen an increase in violent crime, particularly gang-related violence. Some areas of Ponce, particularly around the outskirts, have higher crime rates. The city itself, however, is generally safe in tourist-friendly areas.

**Caguas,** located in the central region, has been dealing with similar crime issues as the other urban areas, such as drug trafficking and street violence. Visitors should exercise caution in less-developed neighborhoods.

While the **rural areas** of Puerto Rico can be stunning, they can also harbor isolated pockets of crime, including thefts and drug-related activity. These areas are typically less patrolled, so it's advisable for visitors to be cautious and avoid venturing into unfamiliar or poorly lit areas after dark.

Crime metrics, including property crimes and violent offenses, can fluctuate greatly depending on the specific location. Puerto Rico's crime patterns are largely **driven by socio-economic** issues such as poverty and limited opportunities, which are also present in economically challenged areas on the U.S. mainland and often contribute to higher crime rates.

While Puerto Rico is a U.S. territory and generally not subject to the same travel advisories as foreign countries, it is still a good idea to consult the **U.S. Department of State's Travel Advisory** website for the latest information on crime and safety tips. For health and safety updates, especially regarding natural disasters, public health, or ongoing concerns, the **Centers for Disease Control and Prevention (CDC)** is a helpful resource.

## Crime Statistics

When comparing Puerto Rico's crime rates to global averages, the situation becomes more contextual. As of recent years, Puerto Rico's **homicide rate** stands at approximately **16.5 per 100,000 people**, which is relatively high compared to the U.S. mainland's average of about 6.5. However, it is still much lower than some of its Caribbean neighbors, such as Jamaica and the Dominican Republic, where violent crime rates are often higher. Puerto Rico's violent crime rate is also lower than several regions in Latin America, which tend to have higher rates of crime, especially in countries like Venezuela and Honduras.

In terms of **petty crime**, Puerto Rico's **rates are higher** than those in many Western countries but still comparatively lower than in other Caribbean or Latin American nations with significant tourist traffic, such as the Dominican Republic and Mexico, which experience higher rates of street crime and armed robberies in tourist areas. While Puerto Rico does experience incidents of petty theft, tourists in popular areas like Old San Juan and Condado are generally safe, provided they take precautions.

Puerto Rico benefits from **strong law enforcement**, with local police and specialized units like the **Tourism Police** working to maintain public safety, particularly in tourist-heavy areas. The island also enjoys political stability as a U.S. territory, allowing law enforcement to focus resources on policing and maintaining public order. However, like many tourist destinations, the increasing number of visitors can sometimes make Puerto Rico a target for opportunistic crimes, particularly petty theft in crowded areas.

 **Quick Safety Tips**

- Popular tourist spots like Old San Juan and beaches can attract pickpockets. **Keep an eye on your belongings and avoid leaving valuables unattended.**

- While many areas are safe, it's **best to avoid walking alone in unfamiliar neighborhoods or poorly lit streets after dark.** Use taxis or rideshare services like Uber when possible.

- Use hotel safes to store important items like passports, credit cards, and extra cash. When out, **carry only what you need and keep it in a front pocket or money belt.**

- Stick to licensed taxis, rideshare services, or rental cars from trusted agencies. **Avoid unmarked taxis or accepting rides from strangers.**

- While Puerto Rico offers beautiful landscapes, some rural or isolated areas can be less safe. **Stick to well-traveled routes, especially if hiking or exploring off the beaten path.**

- If something feels off or uncomfortable, **trust your gut.** Move to a safer location or ask locals for advice if you're unsure about an area.

CHAPTER 4

# CRIMINAL LAW VIOLATIONS

# CRIMINAL LAW VIOLATIONS

## Marijuana and Other Drugs in Puerto Rico

Historically, marijuana has been illegal in Puerto Rico, as it has been across much of the United States. For many years, cannabis was viewed primarily through the lens of prohibition, and penalties for possession, distribution, and cultivation were harsh. However, the island's **cannabis policies began to shift in the last decade**, following trends seen in many U.S. states that began to reevaluate their laws.

This shift was especially noticeable in the mid-2010s, when the Puerto Rican government began to explore the medical uses of cannabis. In **2015**, Puerto Rico **legalized medical marijuana** under the Act 42, which created a regulatory framework for patients with qualifying conditions such as chronic pain, cancer, epilepsy, and post-traumatic stress disorder (PTSD). As part of this law, medical marijuana patients can obtain cannabis through licensed dispensaries with a doctor's prescription. The law also allows the use of cannabis in various forms, such as oils, edibles, tinctures, and smokable marijuana, though smoking in public places is still prohibited.

On the other hand, **recreational marijuana** use remains **illegal** in Puerto Rico. The possession of marijuana for recreational purposes can result in fines or, in more severe cases, criminal charges. Law enforcement continues to treat marijuana use for recreational purposes as a violation of the law, and there are no signs of immediate plans to decriminalize or legalize it for recreational use in the near future, unlike several U.S. states where recreational cannabis has been legalized.

While there has been growing public support for the legalization of recreational cannabis in Puerto Rico, the island's stance remains in line with federal U.S. law, where **marijuana is still classified as a Schedule I controlled substance**, and the possession, cultivation, and sale are considered felonies, which can be punished by up to five years in prison and US$5,000 in fines on the first offense.[5]

Additionally, the economic impact of a potential legalization for recreational use has been a point of debate, with supporters advocating for tax revenue and job creation, while opponents cite concerns over public health and safety.

*Synthetic Cannabinoids*

Puerto Rico's legislative stance on **synthetic cannabinoids** is firmly rooted in the **Controlled Substances Act**, which specifically addresses the dangers these substances pose to public health. Synthetic cannabinoids, often sold under names like "Spice" or "K2," are chemically related to tetrahydrocannabinol (THC) derived from cannabis but can have unpredictable and dangerous effects on users, including severe health crises and mental health issues. Recognizing the risks, Puerto Rico explicitly included synthetic cannabinoids in the Controlled Substances Act in 2011, making it **illegal to manufacture, distribute, or sell** these substances. This inclusion places synthetic cannabinoids under the same legal framework as other narcotics, highlighting the government's proactive approach to safeguarding public health.[6]

---

5   https://www.health-street.net/marijuana-compliance/
    puerto-rico-marijuana-compliance/

6   https://casetext.com/statute/laws-of-puerto-rico/title-twen-
    ty-four-health-and-sanitation/part-v-controlled-substances/
    chapter-111-controlled-substances-act-of-puerto-rico

## Other Illegal Drugs

Puerto Rico's stance on **other illegal drugs** is **aligned with U.S. federal law**, as it is a U.S. territory. The island enforces strict regulations on the possession, distribution, and use of illegal substances. Here's an overview of how Puerto Rico handles various drugs:

**Cocaine** is classified as a **Schedule II controlled substance** under both U.S. federal and Puerto Rican law. Possession, trafficking, or distribution of cocaine carries severe penalties, including **prison sentences**, **large fines**, and **long-term criminal records**. Sentences for trafficking can be especially harsh, with mandatory minimum sentences depending on the quantity involved.

Like cocaine, **heroin** is a **Schedule I controlled substance** due to its high potential for abuse and addiction. Possessing or distributing heroin in Puerto Rico is illegal and can result in severe legal consequences, including **prison time** and **criminal charges**. The island has been combating the opioid crisis, which includes heroin abuse, with public health campaigns and stricter regulations.

**Methamphetamine**, often referred to as **meth**, is also **illegal** in Puerto Rico. It is classified as a **Schedule II controlled substance**, similar to cocaine. Possession, manufacturing, or distribution of methamphetamine can lead to **heavy criminal penalties**, including **long prison sentences**. Puerto Rico has made significant efforts to combat methamphetamine production and distribution, particularly in areas where drug trafficking organizations are active.

**Hallucinogens**, including **LSD** and **psilocybin mushrooms**, are **illegal** in Puerto Rico. These substances are classified as **Schedule I drugs**, which means they are considered to have a high potential for abuse and no accepted medical use. Possessing, using, or distributing hallucinogens is a criminal offense and can result in significant legal penalties, including **prison sentences**.

**Other illegal psychoactive substances**, such as **ecstasy** (MDMA), are also prohibited. Like hallucinogens, they are treated as **Schedule I drugs**

and possessing or trafficking in these substances can result in **criminal charges, fines,** and **incarceration.**

## Penalties

In Puerto Rico, drug-related offenses are treated with **strict penalties,** particularly when it comes to the **possession, trafficking,** or **distribution** of marijuana, synthetic cannabinoids, and other illicit drugs. The penalties vary based on the type and amount of drug involved, as well as the specific circumstances of the crime. Here's an overview of the legal consequences for drug offenses in Puerto Rico:

*Marijuana Penalties:*

- **Possession of Small Amounts:** For possession of small amounts of marijuana, typically **under 1 ounce** (around 28 grams), offenders may face fines up to **US$500.** However, in some cases, first-time offenders may be subject to **warnings** or **community service** instead of jail time. For repeat offenders or larger amounts, penalties may include **imprisonment.**

- **Trafficking or Distribution:** If caught trafficking or distributing marijuana, the penalties become more severe. The sentence for trafficking marijuana can range from **6 to 20 years in prison,** depending on the amount of marijuana and the circumstances of the offense. This includes penalties for **cultivating marijuana** for commercial purposes.

- **Cultivation:** Growing marijuana is also illegal in Puerto Rico, and penalties for cultivation can be equivalent to those for trafficking. The severity of the penalty depends on the scale of cultivation, with **fines and prison sentences** for those found growing marijuana in large quantities.

*Synthetic Cannabinoids Penalties*

- **Possession:** Possessing synthetic cannabinoids, often sold under names like "Spice" or "K2," is illegal in Puerto Rico. Possession can lead to penalties similar to those for other illegal substances, typically including fines or prison sentences of up to 3 years, depending on the amount and context of the offense.

- **Trafficking:** Trafficking or distributing synthetic cannabinoids is a serious offense in Puerto Rico. Individuals caught trafficking synthetic cannabinoids can face severe penalties ranging from 6 to 20 years in prison, depending on the scale of trafficking and the quantity involved.

## *Penalties for Other Drugs:*

### *Cocaine:*

- **Possession:** Possession of even small amounts of cocaine in Puerto Rico can result in significant penalties. Possessing **small quantities (less than 1 gram)** can lead to **3 to 5 years in prison**, while larger quantities could lead to much longer sentences.
- **Trafficking:** Cocaine trafficking is heavily penalized in Puerto Rico. Individuals convicted of trafficking cocaine may face **prison sentences ranging from 10 to 20 years**, or even life imprisonment for large-scale trafficking operations.

### *Methamphetamines & Heroin:*

- **Possession:** Possession of methamphetamines or heroin can lead to prison sentences ranging from **3 to 5 years** for **small quantities**. Larger amounts can result in significantly longer sentences, up to **20 years or more**.
- **Trafficking or Distribution:** Trafficking methamphetamines or heroin carries **severe penalties**, often ranging from **6 to 20 years** in prison, depending on the amount involved and whether the defendant was part of a larger trafficking organization.

*Ecstasy (MDMA), LSD, and Club Drugs:*

- Possessing **club drugs** like **ecstasy** (**MDMA**), **LSD**, or other psycho-active substances can result in **fines** or **imprisonment for up to 3 years** for personal use.
- **Trafficking** in these drugs is treated with equal severity, and penalties for distribution can range from **6 to 20 years** in prison.

*Other Legal Considerations:*

- **Trafficking:** If convicted of trafficking any illicit drug, whether marijuana, synthetic cannabinoids, or other narcotics, the penalty can range from 6 to 20 years in prison, or even longer in extreme cases. The severity depends on the quantity, the method of trafficking, and whether it involves organized crime networks.
- **Drug Use in Public:** Using drugs, including marijuana (even for medical use), in public places is prohibited and can lead to arrest or fines. Public drug use is particularly scrutinized in tourist-heavy areas where law enforcement is more active.
- **Foreign Nationals:** Foreigners caught with drugs in Puerto Rico face the same legal consequences as Puerto Rican citizens. In addition to criminal charges, foreign nationals may also face deportation and banishment from entering Puerto Rico or the U.S. mainland in the future if convicted of drug-related crimes.

## Prescription Medication[7]

When traveling to Puerto Rico, the rules for bringing **prescription medication** largely follow **U.S. federal regulations**, since Puerto Rico is a U.S. territory. If you're bringing prescription drugs for personal use, the key is to ensure you're well-prepared. It's important to carry the medication in its **original packaging with clear labels**, including your name, the prescribing doctor's details, and dosage instructions. Additionally,

---

7    https://wwwnc.cdc.gov/travel/destinations/puerto-rico/traveler/
      packing-list

having a **doctor's note or the original prescription** can help avoid confusion, especially if you're carrying controlled substances like painkillers or anxiety medications, which are regulated more strictly. Without proper documentation, you could face delays or complications at customs.

For **over-the-counter medications**, the regulations are generally more lenient. Medications like ibuprofen, aspirin, and antihistamines are typically fine, but some medications that are available freely in other countries might be restricted in Puerto Rico. This includes certain cold medications containing pseudoephedrine, which could be flagged due to its potential misuse in the production of illegal drugs like methamphetamine.

However, there are **penalties** if you bring **illicit substances** or **unapproved drugs** into Puerto Rico. If you fail to declare controlled medications or attempt to bring illegal drugs into the territory, your medications could be **seized**, and you might face **fines** or even **criminal charges. If you're carrying a controlled substance without the necessary documentation, the consequences could be severe, ranging from fines to more serious legal repercussions.**

To avoid any issues, it's **always wise to check with U.S. Customs and Border Protection** or consult the Puerto Rican authorities if you're unsure about a specific medication before your trip. By following the rules and carrying the proper documentation, you can ensure that your travel with prescription or over-the-counter medications goes smoothly.

## General Questions

1. *Is cannabis legal in Puerto Rico?* **Yes**. Cannabis is **legal for medical** use in Puerto Rico, but **recreational cannabis** remains **illegal**. In 2015, Puerto Rico passed the Medical Cannabis Act, allowing patients with qualifying medical conditions to access cannabis with a prescription. The law allows for the cultivation, sale, and use of cannabis for medicinal purposes, but it is strictly regulated by the Puerto Rico Department of Health.

2. *Where can I legally purchase marijuana in Puerto Rico?* You can legally purchase **medical marijuana** in Puerto Rico at **licensed dispensaries**. These dispensaries are regulated by the Puerto Rico Department of Health, and only individuals who have been issued a medical marijuana card (through a qualified healthcare provider) can purchase cannabis products. There are several dispensaries across the island, particularly in more urban areas like **San Juan**. The purchase of **recreational marijuana** is prohibited, and any attempt to buy or possess marijuana without a medical prescription can result in legal consequences.

3. *Can I have marijuana on my person or in my hotel room in Puerto Rico?* In Puerto Rico, if you are a **medical marijuana** patient **with a valid prescription, you can legally carry marijuana on your person or keep it in your hotel room for personal use**. However, public consumption is prohibited, and you must follow possession limits (usually a 30-day supply). Additionally, many hotels may have their own policies regarding cannabis use, so it's important to check with the hotel beforehand. Smoking or using marijuana in public areas, including beaches and parks, is not allowed.

4. *Are there any other exceptions to the possession and consumption of cannabis in Puerto Rico?* **No.** Besides medical cannabis, there are no other exceptions to the possession or consumption of cannabis in Puerto Rico. Recreational use remains illegal, and the territory does not have provisions for decriminalization or other exceptions outside of medical use. Possessing or consuming cannabis for non-medical purposes can result in legal consequences, including fines or criminal charges.

5. *What are the penalties for possessing and consuming other types of illicit drugs in Puerto Rico?* In Puerto Rico, the penalties for possessing and consuming illicit drugs are severe. **Possession of small amounts** of drugs like cocaine, heroin, or methamphetamines can lead to fines or prison sentences ranging from **3 to 5 years. Public consumption** of illicit drugs is also prohibited and can result in **fines and arrest. Possession with intent to distribute** is treated as a more serious offense, leading to **longer prison sentences.** Foreign nationals caught with illegal drugs face the same penalties as locals, including possible deportation.

 **Law of the Land Hypothetical**

**HYPOTHETICAL**: *Maria, a tourist visiting Puerto Rico, is caught with a small amount of cocaine (less than 5 grams) in her possession while walking through a popular area in San Juan. She explains that she was not intending to sell or distribute the drug and that she had it for personal use. The police arrest her on the spot and take her to the station for questioning. What are the possible legal consequences for Maria in Puerto Rico, and what defenses might she have against the drug possession charge?*

**ANSWER**: *In Puerto Rico, cocaine possession is a serious offense, regardless of the amount. Since Maria was caught with a small quantity, she is facing a potential prison sentence of 3 to 5 years for simple possession* of illicit drugs under local drug laws. Even though she claims the co- caine was for personal use, it's important to note that possession of illegal drugs, even for personal consumption, is still illegal and subject to severe penalties.

As a defense, Maria might argue that she did not intend to distribute the drug, which could be a mitigating factor. However, the law does not differentiate between personal use and distribution when it comes to the initial charge of possession. If she were caught in possession with intent to distribute (such as carrying drug paraphernalia or large amounts), the penalties would be far more severe. As a foreign tour- ist, Maria could also face deportation after serving any sentence, in addition to the prison time. In some cases, the court might consider re- ducing her sentence if she is a first-time offender or if she demonstrates remorse, but this would depend on the specific circumstances and the judge's discretion.

## Takeaways

- Cannabis is **legal** in Puerto Rico **for medical use**, allowing pa- tients with qualifying conditions like chronic pain, cancer, and PTSD to obtain it through licensed dispensaries with a doctor's prescription. However, recreational cannabis use remains illegal.

- Possessing marijuana for recreational use can result in fines or criminal charges, and there are no immediate plans to decriminal- ize or legalize it. Marijuana is still classified as a Schedule I con- trolled substance under U.S. federal law, influencing Puerto Rico's laws.

- Puerto Rico has banned synthetic cannabinoids (e.g., "Spice" or "K2") under its Controlled Substances Act. These substances are illegal to manufacture, sell, or distribute due to the health risks they pose.

- Puerto Rico follows U.S. federal law, making cocaine, heroin, methamphetamines, and hallucinogens illegal. Possession and trafficking of these drugs carry severe penalties, including long prison sentences, fines, and criminal records.

- Foreign tourists caught with illegal drugs in Puerto Rico face the same penalties as locals, including potential deportation and a ban from entering Puerto Rico or the U.S. mainland.

# ALCOHOL-RELATED OFFENSES

# ALCOHOL-RELATED OFFENSES

## Alcohol-Related Offenses

Alcohol holds a significant place in Puerto Rican culture, deeply rooted in the island's colonial past and the local traditions that have developed over centuries. Spanish influences, combined with the Caribbean lifestyle, have **made rum a cultural symbol of Puerto Rico**, with iconic drinks like **Piña Coladas, Cuba Libres**, and **Mojitos** being widely consumed both on the island and abroad.

Alcohol is commonly enjoyed in social settings—whether at bars, family gatherings, or public festivals—where it plays a role in bonding and celebration. However, while alcohol is an integral part of daily life, Puerto Rican society places a **strong emphasis on moderation**, and the social norms around drinking encourage responsible behavior.

The island has a broad range of establishments where alcohol can be purchased and consumed, from street-side kiosks to high-end restaurants and popular bars in tourist hotspots. **Public drinking**, however, is **regulated. Alcohol is only permitted in authorized areas, and public intoxication or disorderly behavior can result in fines or arrest.**

The laws surrounding alcohol consumption also address safety concerns, with stringent regulations on driving under the influence. DUI offenses are taken very seriously, and **law enforcement actively monitors roads, particularly in tourist-heavy areas, to deter reckless driving.**

Additionally, underage drinking is prohibited, and **public intoxication** and **disorderly conduct** due to alcohol use can also **lead to arrests**. In tourist zones, where alcohol consumption is often more visible, authorities are especially vigilant in maintaining public order and safety.

While alcohol is deeply woven into Puerto Rican life and culture, the island's legal framework reflects a commitment to promoting responsible drinking, public safety, and the well-being of residents and visitors alike. Alcohol-related offenses, particularly those linked to driving or disruptive behavior, are treated with serious legal consequences to ensure a safe and enjoyable environment for everyone.

### *Typical Puerto Rican Drinks*

**Rum**, particularly Puerto Rican rum, is arguably the most iconic alcoholic drink associated with the island. Puerto Rico is home to some of the world's top rum brands, such as Don Q and Bacardi, which have become synonymous with the country's drinking culture. Traditional rum drinks such as the **Piña Colada**—made with rum, coconut cream, and pineapple juice—have gained global recognition. Other popular cocktails include the **Cuba Libre** (rum, cola, and lime) and **Mojitos**, which reflect the island's affinity for refreshing rum-based drinks.

Aside from rum, Puerto Ricans enjoy *medallas* (beer), with **Medalla Light** being the most popular local beer. Local wines and cocktails also feature prominently in the island's drinking culture, but rum remains the most iconic and widely consumed alcoholic beverage.

## Alcohol Regulation

Alcohol regulation in Puerto Rico is shaped by both local laws and U.S. federal regulations. As a U.S. territory, Puerto Rico enforces a **legal drinking age of 18**, which is lower than in the mainland U.S. Alcohol is widely available for purchase in bars, restaurants, liquor stores, and local markets, with a prominent rum production industry.

The sale and distribution of alcohol are **regulated by the Puerto Rico Department of Treasury,** which ensures that businesses hold the necessary licenses. Alcohol sales are generally allowed between 7 a.m. and midnight, though this can vary depending on the type of establishment or municipality.

**Driving under the influence** is taken seriously, with a legal blood alcohol concentration (BAC) limit of 0.08 percent and strict penalties for violations. DUI offenders face fines, potential jail time, and mandatory alcohol education programs. Police often set up checkpoints, particularly in tourist areas, to deter drunk driving.

Alcohol-related laws in Puerto Rico are strictly enforced, particularly regarding underage drinking, DUI, public intoxication, and business compliance with alcohol regulations. Authorities, including local police, conduct regular checks and operations to ensure adherence to the legal drinking age, sobriety limits, and responsible alcohol sales. Violations can result in fines, arrests, or business penalties, ensuring that alcohol use is regulated in line with public safety and cultural norms.

 **Things to Remember**

- **Drinking Age:** The legal drinking age is 18.
- **ID:** You need a valid ID to purchase alcohol.
- **Public Consumption:** It is generally illegal to drink alcohol in public places, though exceptions exist for certain designated areas.
- **Public Drunkenness:** Public drunkenness can result in fines or arrest for disruptive behavior.
- **Drunk Driving:** The BAC limit is 0.08 percent, with penalties including fines, license suspension, and possible jail time.
- **Purchase of Alcohol:** Alcohol can be purchased any day, but sales are typically restricted after 10 p.m.

- **Alcohol Permits:** Permits are required for serving or selling alcohol at public events.
- **Illegal Alcohol:** Counterfeit or smuggled alcohol is a concern but not widespread.

 ## General Questions

1. *Can I drink and drive in Puerto Rico?* **No.** You cannot drink and drive in Puerto Rico. The legal blood alcohol concentration (BAC) limit for drivers is 0.08 percent, similar to most U.S. states. Driving under the influence can lead to severe penalties, including fines, license suspension, and jail time.

2. *Can I possess an open container in public?* **No.** It is illegal to possess an open alcohol container in public places in Puerto Rico. Public consumption of alcohol is generally prohibited, though some areas like specific beach zones or private properties may allow it if permitted by local regulations.

 ## Law of the Land Hypothetical

HYPOTHETICAL: *Sarah, a tourist visiting Puerto Rico, is enjoying a sunny afternoon at a popular beach in San Juan with some friends. After purchasing a couple of drinks at a nearby bar, she sits on the beach and starts drinking from an open can of Medalla Light (local beer). While she is sitting on the beach, a police officer approaches and informs her that drinking alcohol on the public beach is prohibited. Can Sarah be fined or arrested for drinking alcohol on the public beach, and what are the potential consequences?*

**ANSWER: Yes.** *Sarah can face legal consequences for drinking alcohol on a public beach in Puerto Rico, as public consumption is generally prohibited unless specifically allowed in designated areas. In this case, she could be fined, and in some situations, arrested if her behavior is disruptive or if she refuses to comply with the officer's request. The fine for public alcohol consumption can vary, but it's important for visitors to know the local regulations and drink only in authorized zones to avoid trouble.*

 **Takeaways**

- The legal drinking age in Puerto Rico is 18, which is lower than in most parts of the U.S. This applies to both residents and visitors.

- Public drinking is generally prohibited, and possessing open alcohol containers in public is illegal. However, certain designated areas or private venues may allow alcohol consumption.

- The legal BAC limit for driving is 0.08 percent, and DUI offenses are taken seriously. Violators face penalties like fines, license suspension, and possible jail time. Police actively monitor roads, especially in tourist areas.

- Alcohol-related laws are strictly enforced, particularly regarding underage drinking, public intoxication, and DUI. Businesses must comply with licensing regulations, and public intoxication can result in fines or arrest for disruptive behavior.

- Alcohol is widely available, with bars, restaurants, and local markets selling it. Sales are generally allowed between 7 a.m. and midnight, though exceptions exist depending on the municipality or establishment type.

CHAPTER 6

# FIREARM & AMMUNITION OFFENSES

# FIREARM & AMMUNITION OFFENSES

## Current Firearm Status[8]

In Puerto Rico, **firearm ownership is tightly regulated by both local and U.S. federal laws,** ensuring that those who own firearms meet stringent requirements aimed at promoting public safety. To legally own a firearm, individuals must be **at least** 21 years old and **must be U.S. citizens or legal residents. Tourists and non-residents are generally not permitted to own firearms in Puerto Rico.** A thorough background check is mandatory, including fingerprinting, to ensure that applicants do not have felony convictions or a history of domestic violence, both of which would disqualify them from firearm ownership. Additionally, individuals must not have been diagnosed with mental illness or have a history of involuntary commitment to a mental health facility.

Firearms that are legally allowed in Puerto Rico include **handguns, rifles,** and **shotguns,** as long as the owner complies with the law. Handguns, both semi-automatic and revolver styles, are commonly owned by residents. Rifles and shotguns, often used for hunting or self-defense, are also legal. However, **military-style rifles and fully automatic weapons are heavily restricted and require special permits for ownership.**

---

8    https://www.usconcealedcarry.com/blog/
     puerto-rico-gun-laws-what-you-need-to-know/

There are no specific limits on how many firearms an individual can possess, but each firearm **must be properly registered with the Puerto Rico Police Department**. The registration process ensures that firearms are accounted for, and owners can be traced if necessary.

## Legal Requirements for Purchasing, Carrying and Using Firearms

**Purchasing a firearm** in Puerto Rico requires a few steps. First, applicants **must apply for a firearm license** from the Puerto Rico Police Department. The application involves a **background check, fingerprinting**, and the **completion of a psychological evaluation** to ensure the applicant is mentally stable and fit to own a weapon. Applicants may also need to **complete a safety and training course**, which includes both written and practical components. The whole process to get the license to possess firearms can take up to 45 days.[9]

If someone wishes to carry a firearm in public, they must apply for a **concealed carry permit**, which involves a **more rigorous application process** than for ownership alone. **Open carry**, on the other hand, is **generally prohibited except** for law enforcement officers and certain licensed security personnel. Regardless of whether a firearm is being bought, sold, or transferred, it must always be properly registered with the Puerto Rico Police Department.[10]

In Puerto Rico, a firearm license generally costs around **US$200 for a gun ownership license** and between **US$300 to $500 for a concealed carry license. Renewal fees** typically range from **US$100 to $200**. Additional costs may include fingerprinting (about US$25 to $50) and training courses (around US$50 to $100). It's important to check with local authorities for the most current fees.

---

9   https://blackbasin.com/laws/puerto-rico/?srsltid=AfmBOooewAPUy-ldHMVpOUv9T69nmkZQAGGItg44m2-_qLrOiKeB0dmtU

10   https://www.usconcealedcarry.com/resources/ccw_reciprocity_map/pr-gun-laws/

The **Puerto Rico Weapons Act of 2020** regulates the use of firearms in Puerto Rico. The legislation is **stringent** and focuses heavily on ensuring public safety. The use of a firearm is **primarily allowed for self-defense or defense of others** in situations where there is an immediate and reasonable threat to life. Puerto Rico follows a **"stand-your-ground"** approach, meaning individuals have the right to use deadly force if they believe they are in danger, without the obligation to retreat. However, the use of force must be proportional to the threat.

Outside of self-defense, the use of firearms is heavily restricted. **Discharging a firearm in public** without just cause, such as for intimidation or recklessness, is a **serious criminal offense** that can result in severe penalties, including imprisonment. The possession and use of firearms are closely regulated, and carrying a firearm in public requires a concealed carry license, which can only be obtained through a thorough application process.

## Firearm Restrictions for Visitors

Non-citizens in Puerto Rico are subject to **strict firearm restrictions**. They **generally cannot possess or carry firearms** unless they are law enforcement officers or military personnel. Visitors are prohibited from carrying firearms in public, and any temporary importation of firearms, such as for hunting or sport shooting, must comply with federal regulations and obtain necessary permits from the Puerto Rico Police Department. Additionally, U.S. visitors cannot carry firearms in Puerto Rico, even with a concealed carry permit from another state, as Puerto Rico does not recognize out-of-state permits. To legally carry a firearm in Puerto Rico, visitors would need to obtain a separate Puerto Rican license.

Visitors are required to adhere to **additional regulations** when traveling with firearms, including providing a written notice to the Puerto Rico Police Bureau five business days prior to their arrival. This notice is essential for ensuring that the travel and declaration of firearms comply with local laws.[11] **Upon entering the territory, non-residents must also inform local law enforcement of their intent to carry,** ensuring that all guidelines are followed during their stay.

However, visitors should be aware that they are still subject to regulations regarding where they can carry firearms. Prohibited locations include schools, government buildings, and private properties where firearms are banned. **Visitors' rights may also be limited in the event of criminal activity; engaging in actions deemed illegal can lead to the revocation of any firearm permits.**

 **Penalties**

In Puerto Rico, firearm-related offenses carry severe penalties, reflecting the territory's strict gun control laws. The penalties vary depending on the type of violation, but some key firearm-related offenses and their associated penalties include:

### Illegal Possession of a Firearm:

- Possessing a firearm without the proper license or permit is a **felony** offense.

- Penalties can include **up to 10 years of imprisonment** and significant fines.

### Carrying a Firearm Without a License:

- Carrying a firearm in public without a valid concealed carry license is also a **felony.**

---

11   https://www.usconcealedcarry.com/blog/
     puerto-rico-gun-laws-what-you-need-to-know

- Penalties can range from **2 to 5 years of imprisonment** and/or fines, depending on the circumstances.

## Illegal Discharge of a Firearm:

- Discharging a firearm in a public space without justification (e.g., for intimidation, recklessness, or in areas where firearms are prohibited) can result in **up to 10 years of imprisonment**.

- If someone is injured or killed as a result of the discharge, the penalties could be even more severe.

## Possession of Firearms by Felons or Prohibited Persons:

- Convicted felons or individuals who are legally prohibited from owning firearms (e.g., those with restraining orders or certain mental health conditions) caught in possession of a firearm face mandatory imprisonment.

- Penalties can range from 5 to 10 years in prison, and in some cases, the firearm may be confiscated.

## Use of a Firearm in a Crime:

- Using a firearm during the commission of a crime (such as robbery, assault, or murder) significantly increases the severity of penalties.

- The use of a firearm in a violent crime can lead to **enhanced sentences**, including **lengthy prison terms** and possible life sentences in the case of homicide.

## Illegal Transfer or Sale of Firearms:

- Selling or transferring firearms illegally, including to individuals who are prohibited from possessing them, is a **felony** offense.

- Penalties can include **up to 10 years of imprisonment** and fines.

## Carrying a Firearm in Prohibited Areas:

- Carrying a firearm in places where it is explicitly prohibited, such as schools, government buildings, or private property with no fire-arms allowed, is subject to penalties.

- This can result in fines and/or imprisonment, typically ranging from **1 to 5 years**, depending on the offense.

## Unlawful Use of Firearms in Domestic Violence Cases:

- If a firearm is used in the commission of domestic violence or against a person protected by a restraining order, the penalties can be particularly severe.

- Penalties include **mandatory imprisonment** and the potential loss of firearm rights.

 **General Questions**

1. *What happens if the police catch me carrying a firearm in Puerto Rico?* If the police catch you carrying a firearm in Puerto Rico without a valid license, **you will likely be arrested, and the firearm will be confiscated.** You will face criminal charges for illegal possession of carrying a firearm. An investigation will follow, and depending on the situation, you may be detained until your court hearing.

2. *What is the potential sentence for a firearms violation upon conviction?* The sentence for a firearms violation in Puerto Rico depends on the offense, but convictions can lead to significant penalties. Carrying a firearm without a license can result in 2 to 5 years in prison. Illegal possession may lead to 3 to 10 years. Discharging a firearm unlawfully can be up to 10 years in prison and using a firearm in a crime can result in enhanced penalties, including life sentences. Other violations, like illegal firearm sales, can also lead to long prison terms.

 **Law of the Land Hypothetical**

HYPOTHETICAL: *Carlos, a U.S. citizen who recently moved to Puerto Rico for work, is visiting a friend's house in San Juan. He brought along his concealed carry firearm, which is legally registered in his home state of Florida. While at his friend's house, Carlos is confronted by a group of individuals outside who seem to be engaging in a hostile argument with him. Fearing for his safety, Carlos decides to draw his weapon to defend himself. Can Carlos legally carry and use a firearm in Puerto Rico, given that he holds a valid concealed carry license from another state in the U.S.?*

ANSWER: **No.** *Carlos cannot legally carry and use his firearm in Puerto Rico, even though he holds a valid concealed carry permit from Florida. Puerto Rico does not recognize out-of-state permits. Non-residents must obtain a separate firearm license from the Puerto Rico Police Department, which involves background checks, fingerprinting, and training. Although Puerto Rico has a "stand-your-ground" law, allowing self-defense with deadly force, Carlos's failure to have a valid Puerto Rican license means he could face felony charges for carrying a firearm without a permit. Penalties for such an offense include 2 to 5 years of imprisonment, and the unlawful discharge of a firearm could lead to additional charges.*

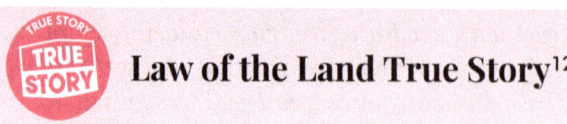

## Law of the Land True Story[12]

The indictment of Ángel Javier Avilés-Monzón for firearms violations sheds light on a larger issue of illegal firearm possession and violence in Puerto Rico, which continues to be a significant concern for both law enforcement and local communities. According to the federal indictment, Avilés-Monzón was charged with possessing a machine gun—an automatic firearm—which is highly regulated under both federal and local laws. This case highlights the growing prevalence of illegal firearms in Puerto Rico, including the rise of military-grade weapons in the hands of individuals involved in criminal activity.

Puerto Rico has long struggled with the problem of gun violence, which is often exacerbated by the availability of illegal firearms. The possession of fully automatic weapons like the one Avilés-Monzón is accused of possessing, which can fire multiple rounds with a single pull of the trigger, escalates the danger to both law enforcement and the general public. The fact that this weapon was modified for automatic fire raises concerns about the ease with which criminals can acquire and alter firearms for illegal use.

In the broader context, Puerto Rico has faced a surge in violence linked to organized crime, with guns being a central tool for criminal gangs. The federal government's increasing focus on firearm-related crimes, as seen in this case, underscores the need for continued vigilance and enhanced cooperation between local and federal agencies to address both the supply and demand for illegal weapons.

---

12  https://www.justice.gov/usao-pr/pr/
    man-indicted-and-arrested-firearms-violations

 **Takeaways**

- To legally own or carry a firearm in Puerto Rico, individuals must meet strict requirements, including background checks, finger-printing, and psychological evaluations. Visitors must obtain a separate Puerto Rican permit to carry.

- A concealed carry permit is required for public firearm possession, and open carry is generally prohibited. Non-residents must apply for a Puerto Rican license, even with a valid out-of-state permit.

- Firearm violations carry serious penalties. Carrying a firearm without a license can lead to 2 to 5 years in prison, while illegal possession or use in a crime can result in up to 10 years or more.

- Puerto Rico follows "stand-your-ground" laws, allowing deadly force in self-defense without retreat. However, force must be pro-portional, and all firearm licensing requirements must be met.

CHAPTER 7

# PROSTITUTION

## IN THIS CHAPTER

- Overview
- Laws and Penalties
- Prostitution Practices
- Sex Trafficking and Exploitation
- Sex Tourism and Public Health
- Tips to Avoid Being Solicited
- Law of the Land Hypothetical
- Takeaways

CHAPTER 7

# PROSTITUTION

## Overview

Prostitution is a **significant issue** in Puerto Rico, largely due to a combination of socio-economic factors and its status as a tourist destination. The sex trade is prevalent, particularly in major tourist areas like San Juan, where sex tourism is a concern. Poverty, unemployment, economic inequality, and drug addiction contribute to individuals, often women, turning to sex work as a means of survival.

In addition to local demand, Puerto Rico also faces problems with **human trafficking**, both for sex work and labor, which further complicates the situation. While prostitution itself is not illegal, activities surrounding it, like pimping and operating brothels, are criminalized, making it difficult to address the issue comprehensively.

Efforts to tackle the problem have focused on raising awareness, combating trafficking, and improving the health and safety of sex workers, but it remains a persistent challenge. The conversation around decriminalization and better protections for sex workers continues, though systemic socio-economic issues still drive many individuals into the trade.

 **Laws and Penalties**

Prostitution itself is **not explicitly illegal** in Puerto Rico, meaning that the exchange of sex for money is not criminalized. However, several **related activities are illegal** and regulated under Puerto Rican law, including:

- **Solicitation** (offering or attempting to purchase sex)
- **Pimping** or **operating a brothel**
- **Human trafficking** for sexual exploitation
- **Sexual exploitation of minors**

These laws are in place to prevent the exploitation of individuals involved in sex work and to combat organized criminal activities surrounding prostitution. While the act of prostitution itself is not illegal, those involved in the **organization**, **promotion**, or **coercion** of prostitution can face criminal charges.

Penalties for prostitution-related infractions in Puerto Rico are as follows: **Solicitation**, which involves offering or attempting to purchase sex, is considered a **misdemeanor** and can result in **fines or up to one year in prison**. **Operating a brothel or pimping** is a **felony** offense, punishable by **3 to 6 years** in prison, along with potential fines. **Human trafficking** and **sexual exploitation**, particularly of minors, carry severe penalties, with sentences **up to 25 years** in prison for trafficking and **life imprisonment** in extreme cases involving minors. **Engaging in prostitution in prohibited areas**, such as near schools, can result in **fines and/or imprisonment** ranging from **1 to 5 years**. While sex workers themselves are generally not penalized, related activities like solicitation and trafficking carry significant legal consequences.

There are **no designated legal areas for prostitution**, meaning that there are no official zones or red-light districts where prostitution is legally permitted or regulated. Puerto Rico does not have specific **legal protections or requirements** for sex workers themselves. Unlike some other regions, there is no regulatory framework that requires licensing or registration for individuals involved in sex work. This leaves sex workers vulnerable to exploitation, as they do not have the legal protections or rights typically afforded to other workers. However, **public health measures are in place**, and there are initiatives aimed at providing **healthcare services to sex workers**, such as HIV/AIDS prevention and other sexual health resources, but these are generally **voluntary** and not mandated by law.

Police routinely enforce laws against prostitution-related activities, especially solicitation in public spaces (near schools, government buildings, etc.). However, law enforcement efforts focus more on cracking down on visible prostitution activities, particularly in tourist-heavy areas, rather than creating regulatory zones.

## Prostitution Practices

Reliable and comprehensive statistics on prostitution in Puerto Rico are hard to come by, as **much of the activity occurs in the underground economy**. However, local reports and observations suggest that prostitution is a **persistent issue** in certain parts of the island, particularly in San Juan and tourist-heavy areas. According to certain local advocacy organizations, a significant portion of individuals involved in prostitution in Puerto Rico are victims of trafficking or forced into sex work due to financial hardships. Law enforcement and social services continue to monitor and address these issues, though accurate statistics remain elusive.

In Puerto Rico, prostitution manifests in **several forms**, each with different levels of visibility and risk. **Street prostitution** is most common in areas like Old San Juan, Condado, and Isla Verde, where individuals work near bars and hotels, often catering to tourists. This form of sex work is linked to higher risks of exploitation and human trafficking. Although **brothels** are illegal, they still exist, typically disguised as private homes, small businesses, or massage parlors. These operations are hidden and often connected to organized crime or sex trafficking, preying on vulnerable individuals.

**Escort services** are prevalent in tourist areas like San Juan, where individuals or agencies advertise through online platforms and local ads.

While some work **independently**, others are controlled by traffickers. This form is less visible than street prostitution but targets affluent clients and can be harder to detect. Lastly, **online prostitution** has grown, with services offered through websites and apps. Though it may appear discreet, it poses significant risks, as traffickers use online spaces to reach broader audiences, blurring the line between consensual sex work and sex trafficking.

Local authorities in Puerto Rico maintain a strict stance against prostitution. Prostitution-related activities, such as solicitation, operating brothels, pimping, and sex trafficking, are criminal offenses, and these crimes are pursued by both **local police** and **federal agencies**, such as **the FBI**, especially in relation to trafficking. Authorities take **a zero-tolerance approach to human trafficking**, which is often tied to prostitution. Over the past decade, there has been an increase in efforts to target traffickers and dismantle illegal networks that exploit individuals for sex. The Puerto Rican government has collaborated with federal agencies and NGOs to improve victim identification and support services for those exploited in prostitution.

However, the **attitude toward sex workers** themselves is more complicated. Many sex workers, particularly those involved in street prostitution or forced into the trade, are viewed as victims rather than criminals. In public health initiatives, there is some recognition of the need to provide medical and psychological support to individuals involved in prostitution, but **stigmatization** and **discrimination** remain significant barriers for sex workers seeking help or services.

## Sex Trafficking and Exploitation[13]

Sex trafficking and exploitation are significant concerns in Puerto Rico. The island has become a **hub for sex trafficking,** partly due to its high tourism rates, geographic location, and economic challenges. Puerto Rico is often viewed as a **transshipment point** for traffickers between

---

13  https://acf.gov/sites/default/files/documents/otip/puerto_rico_profile_
    efforts_to_combat_human_trafficking.pdf

the U.S. mainland, the Caribbean, and Latin America. Traffickers prey on vulnerable populations, exploiting individuals for commercial sex and forced labor. The rise in **sex tourism**, alongside high poverty levels and limited job opportunities, contributes to the growing issue of sex trafficking.

Certain areas of Puerto Rico are more vulnerable to sex trafficking due to factors like tourism, poverty, and socio-economic disparities. Popular tourist destinations like **San Juan**, especially the **Old San Juan** area and beach resort areas, attract both domestic and international tourists, creating conditions where traffickers can more easily operate. **Rural communities** and areas with high poverty rates are also more vulnerable, as traffickers often target marginalized individuals, offering false promises of employment or a better life. The **proximity to international shipping routes** and the **high volume of travelers** moving through airports like **Luis Muñoz Marín International Airport** also contributes to Puerto Rico's vulnerability to sex trafficking.

The demographics most at risk for sex trafficking in Puerto Rico include **young women** and **girls**, particularly those from low-income backgrounds or broken families, as well as **runaways** and **minors** seeking better opportunities. **LGBTQ+ youth** are also highly vulnerable due to social stigma and lack of family support. **Immigrants** and **foreign nationals**, especially from Latin America and the Dominican Republic, are often targeted by traffickers who promise work or a better life but exploit them once they arrive. Additionally, **individuals facing economic hardship**, such as those struggling with poverty, unemployment, or addiction, are more susceptible to trafficking.

 ## Sex Tourism and Public Health

While Puerto Rico is **not globally recognized** as a primary sex tourism destination, like some other regions such as Thailand or the Dominican Republic, **there are areas on the island where sex tourism and sex trafficking are present and have been growing concerns.**

Major tourist hotspots in **San Juan,** particularly in neighborhoods like **Condado, Isla Verde,** and **Old San Juan,** have been identified as areas where sex tourism takes place, often facilitated by traffickers who target vulnerable populations for exploitation. The large number of tourists, especially in areas near resorts and the cruise port, makes it an attractive location for individuals seeking illicit sexual services.

While Puerto Rico may not be internationally branded or marketed as a sex tourism destination, its status as a U.S. territory and its proximity to major U.S. cities, combined with economic vulnerabilities, make it susceptible to sex trafficking and exploitation. Local authorities and NGOs have been working to combat this issue through law enforcement efforts, victim support services, and public awareness campaigns, but the demand for sex work, particularly in tourist-heavy areas, continues to pose challenges.

Sex tourism in Puerto Rico poses significant public health concerns, particularly the transmission of **sexually transmitted infections (STIs),** including **HIV/AIDS.**[14] The high turnover of individuals engaging in sex work, especially in tourist areas, increases the spread of infections, particularly when protection is not used. Sex workers, often with limited access to healthcare, are particularly vulnerable to undiagnosed or untreated conditions. Additionally, the psychological toll on those involved in sex work, particularly trafficked individuals, can lead to mental health issues like PTSD and anxiety. The influx of tourists also contributes to the spread of infections, as safe sex practices are not always followed. Public health organizations are working to raise awareness and improve healthcare access, but the issue remains a significant challenge.

---

14   https://pmc.ncbi.nlm.nih.gov/articles/PMC3667155

 ## Tips to Avoid Being Solicited

If you're traveling in Puerto Rico and want to avoid being solicited by sex workers, here are some practical tips to help you maintain privacy and avoid unwanted attention:

- **Avoid High-Risk Areas:** Steer clear of neighborhoods known for street prostitution, such as parts of Old San Juan, Condado, and Isla Verde—especially at night. These areas are more likely to have individuals actively soliciting clients.

- **Stay in Well-Reviewed Hotels and Resorts:** Choose accommodations with good reputations in safer areas, as high-end hotels or resorts are less likely to have solicitation issues compared to low-budget or poorly reviewed places.

- **Keep a Low Profile:** Avoid engaging in conversation with individuals who approach you on the street, particularly in tourist-heavy areas. Maintaining a low profile and not appearing too eager to interact will help reduce unwanted attention.

- **Use Ride-Sharing Apps:** Instead of hailing a taxi from the street, use ride-sharing apps like Uber or Lyft to avoid being approached by sex workers or traffickers who may target unsuspecting tourists.

- **Respect Local Culture and Social Norms:** Be aware of cultural sensitivities around sex work. Many locals may find solicitation in public places uncomfortable, and being respectful of local norms can help you avoid unwanted attention.

- **Know Local Laws:** Familiarize yourself with the laws regarding prostitution in Puerto Rico so you can recognize when a situation feels inappropriate or illegal. If you feel unsafe or are being harassed, report it to local authorities immediately.

## Law of the Land Hypothetical

HYPOTHETICAL: *Maria, a local resident of Puerto Rico, has been working as a sex worker for several years. She has her own online advertising platform where she offers escort services to clients, primarily in the San Juan area. One day, a new client, John, approaches Maria through her online ad and arranges to meet her at a hotel. After their meeting, John suggests that he could offer her a large sum of money if she agrees to perform certain activities that Maria believes cross a legal boundary under Puerto Rican law.*

*Is Maria at risk of legal trouble for engaging in the activities John has requested, and what legal boundaries should she be aware of under Puerto Rican prostitution laws?*

ANSWER: *Maria could face legal risks if the activities John requests involve illegal acts, such as underage prostitution or exploitation linked to trafficking. While escort services are generally legal in Puerto Rico, engaging in illegal activities, operating like a brothel, or failing to comply with health and safety regulations, could result in criminal charges. Additionally, Maria should ensure that her business adheres to other relevant laws, especially those around public safety, trafficking, and exploitation. She should also be aware of the risks if the activities she engages in go beyond what is legally permissible, particularly regarding consent, safety, and public order, and seek legal advice if unsure about the legality of any requests.*

## Takeaways

- Prostitution is not criminalized, but related activities such as solicitation, pimping, brothel operation, and trafficking are illegal and heavily regulated in Puerto Rico.

- Vulnerable populations, including young women, LGBTQ+ youth, immigrants, and individuals facing economic hardship, are at high risk for sex trafficking and exploitation.

- Sex tourism contributes to the demand for prostitution, particularly in tourist-heavy areas like Old San Juan, Condado, and Isla Verde, making Puerto Rico a hub for trafficking activities.

- Public health risks, including the spread of sexually transmitted infections (STIs), are significant, especially in high-traffic tourist areas where sex work is more visible.

- Law enforcement focuses on combating trafficking and exploitative prostitution practices, but sex workers themselves face limited legal protections, leaving them vulnerable to abuse and exploitation.

CHAPTER 8
# LGBTQ

CHAPTER 8

# LGBTQ

## Homophobia in Puerto Rico

Historically, homosexuality in Puerto Rico was condemned, and LGBTQ+ rights were ignored due to several factors. **Catholicism** remains a dominant force in shaping social norms, with its teachings often condemning same-sex relationships and non-traditional gender roles. These religious views are reinforced by **conservative social structures**, especially in rural areas, where traditional family values are highly prioritized. However, the influence of U.S. media and culture has helped bring more visibility and support for LGBTQ+ rights. LGBTQ activism grew in the 1970s and 1980s, leading to key legal milestones, including the **legalization of same-sex marriage** in **2015**.

Today, LGBTQ+ visibility and acceptance have increased, especially in cities like San Juan, with events like San Juan Pride reflecting a cultural shift. This progress is driven by key figures such as **Pedro Julio Serrano**, a prominent LGBTQ+ activist and founder of *Puerto Rico Para Todes*, an organization dedicated to advocating for LGBTQ+ rights and addressing issues like HIV prevention and anti-trans violence. Similarly, **Bad Bunny**, a global music icon, leverages his fame to challenge traditional gender norms and promote LGBTQ+ inclusivity through his music and public persona.[15]

---

15   https://www.nbcnews.com/nbc-out/out-news/
bad-bunny-eight-trailblazing-queer-icons-puerto-rico-rcna122747

Challenges persist for LGBTQ+ individuals in Puerto Rico, particularly transgender people, who continue to face **discrimination, violence, and opposition** from conservative political and religious groups. In daily life, homophobic attitudes manifest in the workplace, schools, and family settings, where LGBTQ+ individuals often experience **discrimination, bullying**, and **rejection**. Reports of job insecurity, harassment, and pressure to conform to heterosexual norms are common. Violence against LGBTQ+ people, especially transgender individuals, is a significant issue, with **rising hate crimes** and brutal assaults. Despite legal progress, social acceptance remains inconsistent, and many LGBTQ+ individuals still face a hostile environment.

## LGBTQ Legislation

Puerto Rico has implemented several laws that explicitly protect the rights of LGBTQ+ individuals. One of the most notable advancements came in **2015** when **same-sex marriage** was legalized, following the U.S. Supreme Court ruling in *Obergefell v. Hodges*, which mandated that states recognize marriage rights for same-sex couples.[16] This landmark decision has enabled same-sex couples in Puerto Rico to enjoy the same comprehensive rights and benefits that heterosexual couples receive, including those related to taxation, adoption, and healthcare decision-making.

Moreover, **Law No. 22**, passed in **2013**, **prohibits discrimination in employment** based on sexual orientation and gender identity in most public and private sector workplaces. This law aligns Puerto Rico with various states that have enacted similar protections against discrimination, demonstrating a commitment to fostering inclusive work environments for LGBTQ+ individuals. The law also mandates the development of anti-discrimination protocols and training programs, signaling governmental efforts to raise awareness and address biases within workplaces.[17]

---

16   https://www.equaldex.com/region/puerto-rico

17   https://www.oneillborges.com/our_client_alert/
     puerto-rico-prohibits-sexual-orientation-workplace-discrimination

In addition to workplace protections, laws exist that safeguard LGBTQ+ individuals from **discrimination in housing and public accommodations**. Civil rights laws in Puerto Rico explicitly forbid discrimination based on sexual orientation and gender identity in these areas, which is crucial for promoting equality in housing access and public services.[18]

While there has been significant progress, the **legal landscape** in Puerto Rico is **still a mix of supportive and challenging elements for LGBTQ+ individuals**. While laws regarding same-sex marriage, adoption, and anti-discrimination protections are supportive and align with many rights granted in the U.S., **social acceptance** often lags behind legal protections, and discrimination, violence, and stigma against LGBTQ+ individuals, particularly transgender people, remain significant issues. Despite these legal advances, religious and conservative groups continue to push back against full equality, and much work is needed to improve social attitudes and ensure that the legal protections are effectively implemented.

## LGBTQ Tourism and Safety Concerns

LGBTQ+ tourism in Puerto Rico has seen significant growth in recent years, with the island emerging as a popular and **increasingly welcoming destination for LGBTQ+ travelers**. The vibrant LGBTQ+ scene in **San Juan**, particularly in neighborhoods like **Condado** and **Santurce**, offers a variety of LGBTQ+-friendly accommodations, bars, restaurants, and nightlife. Events like **San Juan Pride** and the **Puerto Rico Gay Film Festival** have helped solidify the island's reputation as an inclusive destination. The legal protections for LGBTQ+ individuals, such as same-sex marriage and anti-discrimination laws, also make Puerto Rico a safe and appealing place for LGBTQ+ tourists, especially those traveling from the mainland U.S. looking for an accessible, culturally rich, and LGBTQ+-friendly environment.

However, the **level of acceptance can vary across the island**. In urban centers like **San Juan**, the LGBTQ+ community enjoys a higher degree of visibility and acceptance, with Condado and Santurce standing out

---

18   https://www.discoverpuertorico.com/article/
     lgbtq-travel-guide-to-puerto-rico

as hubs of tolerance. These areas not only host major LGBTQ+ events but also feature an array of businesses catering to the community, from gay-friendly hotels to LGBTQ+ bars and clubs. Smaller islands like **Vieques** and **Culebra** also offer a more relaxed and tolerant atmosphere, making them appealing spots for LGBTQ+ travelers seeking a peaceful and inclusive getaway.

In contrast, **more rural areas and conservative regions of Puerto Rico remain less tolerant.** These areas are often more influenced by traditional family values and the strong presence of Catholicism, which can lead to more homophobic attitudes and a less welcoming environment for LGBTQ+ individuals. In these parts of the island, LGBTQ+ travelers may encounter more discrimination and social resistance, making it important for visitors to be aware of local cultural dynamics.

**Public displays of affection** (PDA) between LGBTQ+ visitors are **generally accepted in urban and tourist-friendly areas**, where LGBTQ+ rights are more visible. However, in more rural or conservative regions, PDA may draw unwanted attention or disapproval, and it's advisable to be more cautious.

Puerto Rico is relatively safe for LGBTQ+ travelers, especially in major tourist areas, thanks to legal protections against discrimination. However, there have been reports of hate crimes, particularly targeting transgender individuals. **Visitors should remain aware of their surroundings and exercise caution in more conservative areas, though safety is generally not a major concern in tourist hubs.**

## General Questions

1. *Do laws in Puerto Rico protect homosexual expressions and conduct?* **Yes.** Laws in Puerto Rico protect homosexual expression and conduct. Same-sex relationships were decriminalized following the U.S. Supreme Court's 2003 decision in Lawrence v. Texas, and the Puerto Rico Supreme Court followed suit. Additionally, Puerto Rico has enacted several laws that provide protections against discrimination based on sexual orientation and gender identity, including in employment, housing, and public accommodations.

2. *What is the punishment for homosexual expressions and conduct?* There are **no punishments** for homosexual expression or conduct in Puerto Rico. Homosexuality is not criminalized, and LGBTQ+ individuals are legally allowed to express their sexual orientation and engage in same-sex relationships without fear of criminal prosecution.

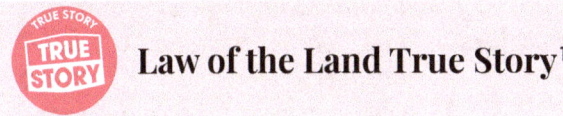

## Law of the Land True Story[19]

Pedro Julio Serrano is one of Puerto Rico's most prominent and controversial human rights activists, particularly known for his work advocating for LGBTQ+ rights. In 1998, as a 24-year-old, he became the island's first openly gay candidate for the Puerto Rican House of Representatives. His candidacy was met with severe hostility, including a death threat in the form of a hateful note and vandalism to his

---

19  https://abcnews.go.com/ABC_Univision/profile-pe-dro-julio-serrano-puerto-ricos-prominent-human/story?id=18458343

car, which symbolized the pervasive anti-LGBTQ+ violence on the island. Despite these challenges, Serrano continued his activism, becoming a key figure in the fight for lesbian, gay, bisexual, and transgender rights in Puerto Rico.

Today, Serrano is a recognized icon in Puerto Rico, drawing both admiration and criticism. He has used modern tools like social media to amplify his messages, reaching over 30,000 followers with frequent posts on Twitter and Facebook, influencing both public opinion and political discourse. Serrano is a strong advocate for gay marriage, hoping to marry in Puerto Rico, and works tirelessly to bring attention to LGBTQ+ hate crimes on the island. Despite the personal toll—often facing hateful comments, bigotry, and exhaustion—he remains committed to his mission of "unteaching" outdated norms and pushing for social change. His work, both in Puerto Rico and beyond, has made him a central figure in the ongoing struggle for LGBTQ+ rights in Puerto Rico.

 **Law of the Land Hypothetical**

HYPOTHETICAL: *Carlos and Javier, a same-sex couple visiting Puerto Rico from the mainland U.S., are on vacation in San Juan. While walking through Condado, they hold hands and share a quick kiss in public. Shortly after, a local resident approaches them and comments negatively, asking them to stop showing affection because it's "inappropriate." Can Carlos and Javier file a complaint or take legal action if they are harassed or asked to stop showing affection in public because they are a same-sex couple?*

ANSWER: **Yes.** *Carlos and Javier can file a complaint if they face harassment. Puerto Rico's anti-discrimination laws protect sexual orientation, so if they are harassed for showing affection, they can report it to the Puerto Rico Civil Rights Commission or pursue legal action. While public displays of affection are generally accepted in places like Condado, social tolerance can vary in more conservative areas. Legal protections are in place, but they may want to be cautious outside of urban hubs.*

CHAPTER 9

# SEXUALLY MOTIVATED/ VIOLENT CRIMES

## IN THIS CHAPTER

- Overview
- Related Legislation
- General Questions
- Law of the Land Hypothetical
- Takeaways

# SEXUALLY MOTIVATED/ VIOLENT CRIMES

## Overview

Sexually motivated crimes in Puerto Rico have been alarmingly high, with estimates indicating that approximately 18,000 individuals, primarily women and girls, fall victim to sexual violence annually.[20] Moreover, the Puerto Rico Police Department has recorded an estimated 679 rapes, though this likely underrepresents the actual number of incidents due to underreporting and insufficient police response.[21]

Several factors contribute to the high incidence of sexual violence, including a deeply ingrained **machismo culture**, **patriarchal societal structures**, and widespread **economic hardship**, with nearly half the population living in poverty. These conditions create an environment where sexual violence is normalized, and victims feel discouraged from reporting.

While sexual violence is a widespread issue on the island, with high rates of abuse, it typically impacts **local residents**, especially **young women**,

20  https://www.aclu.org/documents/
     failure-police-crimes-domestic-violence-and-sexual-assault-puerto-rico

21  https://ucr.fbi.gov/crime-in-the-u.s/2016/crime-in-the-u.s.-2016/tables/
     table-9/table-9-state-cuts/puerto-rico.xls

**bisexual women**, and **LGBTQ+ individuals**, who are disproportionately affected by sexual violence due to social discrimination.

**Tourists are generally not the primary target for sexual crimes**, but they can still be vulnerable, particularly in isolated or less populated areas. The risk of sexual assault can increase if a traveler is in an unfamiliar setting or engaging in risky behaviors such as excessive alcohol consumption. However, tourists visiting well-populated and tourist-friendly areas like San Juan, Condado, or Old San Juan are less likely to be directly targeted, as these areas are heavily policed, and there are greater resources for responding to such incidents.

**While Puerto Rico does not have a specific pattern of targeting tourists for sexual crimes, visitors should still exercise caution, just as they would in any other destination, to ensure their safety and avoid becoming victims of opportunistic crimes.**

## Related Legislation[22]

In Puerto Rico, legislation surrounding sexual violence is relatively robust. The Puerto Rico Penal Code criminalizes rape, sexual assault, and molestation, with significant penalties for perpetrators. For instance, a conviction for rape can lead to a prison sentence ranging from **8 to 15 years**, while **sexual assault** typically carries sentences between **6 to 10 years**. There are also heightened penalties for repeat offenders and cases involving minors or vulnerable individuals.

Additionally, Puerto Rico has implemented comprehensive laws like the **Sexual Exploitation of Children Act**, which targets child sexual exploitation, trafficking, and abuse, with penalties severe enough to include **life imprisonment** for certain offenses. The **Puerto Rico Anti-Discrimination Law** (Law 22) also ensures that individuals, including those in the LGBTQ+ community, are protected against discrimination and violence based on sexual orientation or gender identity. Victims of

---

22  https://apps.rainn.org/policy/policy-crime-definitions.
cfm?state=puerto%20rico&group=3

sexual violence are further protected by legal mechanisms such as **restraining orders** and the **Victim's Compensation Program**, which offers financial assistance for medical care, counseling, and other recovery services.

Yet, despite these protections, enforcement remains inconsistent. One of the key challenges is **underreporting**. Many victims, particularly within marginalized communities like the LGBTQ+ population, often fear stigmatization or doubt that the authorities will respond adequately. This reluctance to report is compounded by a lack of trust in law enforcement, especially in rural or conservative areas. Moreover, Puerto Rico's deeply rooted **machismo culture** and **traditional gender norms** continue to create barriers to both reporting and properly addressing sexual violence. Victims may face cultural pressure to remain silent, and those from marginalized groups may be met with **discrimination** or **victim-blaming** by the police, further discouraging them from seeking help.

While urban areas such as San Juan have seen improvements in law enforcement response and victim support, the situation in rural areas remains more complex, with fewer resources dedicated to sexual violence prevention and victim assistance. The Puerto Rico Police Department, despite efforts to improve, still faces resource constraints, which affects both the investigation of cases and the level of support available to victims.

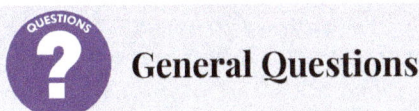

## General Questions

1. *Do laws in Puerto Rico related to sex crimes protect the victims equally?* **Yes**. The laws in Puerto Rico related to sex crimes are designed to protect all victims equally, regardless of gender, sexual orientation, or identity.

2. *Pursuant to law, what is the age of consent for sex in Puerto Rico?* In Puerto Rico, the age of consent for sexual activity is **16 years old**. However, there are exceptions if the adult involved is in a position of authority over the minor, such as a teacher or guardian, which can lead to harsher penalties. Additionally, there are laws in place to protect minors from sexual exploitation and abuse, with more severe penalties for crimes involving children and teenagers under 18.

 **Law of the Land Hypothetical**

HYPOTHETICAL: *Carlos, a 30-year-old tourist from Spain, was sexually assaulted while visiting San Juan, Puerto Rico. He reported the crime to the police and underwent a forensic examination. As a foreigner, Carlos is unsure about his legal rights in Puerto Rico and whether he will be treated differently from local residents. He is concerned about whether the perpetrator can be prosecuted under Puerto Rican law and if Carlos, as a foreigner, has access to the same legal protections and victim support services.*

ANSWER: *In Puerto Rico, there are no special distinctions between local residents and foreign victims of sexually motivated crimes. All individuals, regardless of nationality, are entitled to* **equal legal protection** *under Puerto Rican law. The perpetrator can be prosecuted for sexual assault under the Puerto Rico Penal Code, and Carlos has the same rights as a local victim to pursue justice. Puerto Rican authorities are required to investigate the crime and hold the perpetrator accountable. Carlos also has access to the same victim support services, including the Victim's Compensation Program, which offers financial help for medical care and counseling. While language barriers or cultural differences may arise, Carlos' legal rights are fully protected under Puerto Rican law.*

# Takeaways

- Sexual violence in Puerto Rico is alarmingly high, with many incidents likely to stay unreported due to societal stigma and insufficient police response.

- The majority of sexual violence victims are local residents, with young women, bisexual women, and LGBTQ+ individuals disproportionately affected due to social discrimination and marginalization.

- Puerto Rico has comprehensive laws in place to combat sexual violence, including severe penalties for perpetrators. These laws also protect vulnerable populations and offer victim support services such as the Victim's Compensation Program.

- While tourists are not typically the primary target of sexual violence, they may still be at risk, particularly in isolated areas or when engaging in risky behaviors. Popular tourist areas like San Juan and Old San Juan are generally safer due to heavy policing and resources for handling such incidents.

- Despite strong legal protections, there are challenges in enforcement due to underreporting, lack of trust in law enforcement, and Puerto Rico's deeply ingrained machismo culture. Victims, especially from marginalized groups, may face significant barriers to reporting and accessing justice.

# ARRESTED IN PUERTO RICO

# ARRESTED IN PUERTO RICO

## Overview

When traveling in a foreign country, it's imperative to recognize that you are subject to the legal jurisdiction and regulations of that nation. These laws may significantly differ from those in your home country and might not offer the same legal protections you are accustomed to. It's crucial to bear in mind that penalties for violating foreign laws can be more severe than those for similar offenses in your home country, and ignorance of these laws is not typically accepted as a defense.

The consequences for breaking the law while abroad can be severe and may include expulsion, fines, arrest, or imprisonment. Even unintentional violations can lead to serious legal repercussions. It is essential for travelers to be aware of and adhere to the laws of the host country to avoid legal entanglements and ensure a safe and enjoyable experience.

Specifically, stringent penalties are often enforced for possession, use, or trafficking of illegal drugs in many countries. Convicted offenders can expect severe consequences, including lengthy jail sentences and hefty fines. The legal processes for foreigners in the event of an arrest abroad involve being charged or indicted, prosecuted, potentially convicted and sentenced, and, if applicable, going through an appeals process.

Navigating a foreign legal system can be complex, and individuals arrested abroad must be prepared to comply with the legal procedures of the host country. Seeking legal representation and understanding the local legal nuances are crucial steps for those facing legal issues in a foreign jurisdiction.

Awareness of and adherence to the laws of a foreign country are paramount when traveling. Understanding the potential consequences for legal violations and being prepared to navigate the legal system of the host country are essential aspects of responsible international travel.

## Arrest Process

The arrest process in Puerto Rico is similar to that in the U.S. mainland, as Puerto Rico is a U.S. territory and follows both its own local laws and federal guidelines.

Before an arrest can be made, police must have **probable cause** that a crime has been committed. This can be based on witness testimony, physical evidence, or direct observation of the crime by officers. In some cases, a **warrant** may be required if there is no immediate danger to public safety or if the suspect is not present. If the police have a warrant, they can arrest the individual at their home, workplace, or another location. In urgent cases, such as witnessing a crime in progress or having sufficient evidence that a crime was committed, the police can make an arrest **without a warrant.**

Once the police determine that they have probable cause, they will make the arrest. The **Miranda rights** (right to remain silent and right to an attorney) are read to the suspect at the time of the arrest, as required under U.S. constitutional law. Failure to do so can impact the admissibility of any statements made by the suspect during the arrest. The suspect is taken into custody and transported to a local police station for **booking.**

At the police station, the suspect will go through the **booking** process, which includes:

- Recording personal information (name, date of birth, address, etc.)
- Taking a mugshot

- Fingerprinting
- A background check to determine if there are prior charges or outstanding warrants.

After booking, the suspect is usually brought before a judge within **24 to 48 hours** (depending on the case). The judge will review the evidence and decide whether there is enough cause to charge the suspect and whether the suspect will be granted bail, or if they must remain in custody.

For serious crimes, the judge may deny bail, particularly if there is a risk that the suspect will flee or pose a danger to the community. If granted bail, the suspect may be released pending trial by paying the amount set by the judge.

If the arrest leads to formal charges, the prosecution will file them. From there, the case will move through the legal process, which can involve preliminary hearings, trial, and sentencing (if convicted). Throughout the process, the defendant has the right to legal representation and a fair trial.

**Foreigner visitors** arrested in Puerto Rico are treated similarly to local residents. While there are **no special protections or penalties for foreigners**, there are some considerations. **Language barriers** may arise, but interpreters are provided to ensure understanding. Arrested individuals also have the **right to contact their consulate** for assistance, which can help with legal representation and ensure their rights are upheld. Additionally, if the crime is serious, immigration issues such as deportation could arise. Despite these factors, **foreigners are guaranteed the same legal rights and processes as Puerto Rican citizens.**

## Rights of the Arrested Person[23]

In Puerto Rico, individuals arrested, whether local or foreign, have several legal protections under both Puerto Rican and U.S. federal law. These include:

- **Right to Remain Silent:** The arrested person has the right to remain silent and not incriminate themselves during questioning. This is protected by the U.S. Constitution (5th Amendment).

- **Right to an Attorney:** An arrested person has the right to legal representation. If they cannot afford an attorney, one will be appointed for them (this is the same as in the U.S. under the 6th Amendment).

- **Right to be Informed of Charges:** The arrested person must be informed of the charges against them in a timely manner. This is typically done during the arraignment process, which happens soon after the arrest.

- **Right to a Bail Hearing:** Depending on the charges, the arrested individual may have the right to request bail, although this is not guaranteed for all crimes, especially more severe offenses.

- **Right to a Speedy Trial:** An individual is entitled to a speedy trial, which is meant to prevent prolonged detention without a conviction.

Additionally, individuals are also protected **against unlawful detention** through habeas corpus, ensuring they cannot be held without legal grounds. Detainees are entitled to **humane treatment, access to medical care,** and **protection from torture or inhumane conditions.** Arrested individuals, including foreigners, have the right to a **fair trial**, the presumption of innocence, and the ability to challenge evidence presented against them. Searches and seizures cannot occur without a warrant or probable cause, and minors have special protections under juvenile justice laws. Furthermore, those unable to afford an attorney are entitled to a public defender. These rights are designed to ensure

---

23  https://law.justia.com/codes/puerto-rico/title-twenty-three/part-ii/chapter-29/468/)

that arrested individuals receive a fair process, although the effectiveness of these protections can depend on local practices and specific circumstances.

## Getting Legal Assistance

In Puerto Rico, individuals, including foreign nationals, have the **right to legal counsel** if they are arrested. This right is guaranteed under both U.S. federal law and Puerto Rican law, ensuring that individuals are not deprived of their ability to defend themselves in legal proceedings.

Under the **Sixth Amendment** to the U.S. Constitution, which applies in Puerto Rico, individuals have the right to legal representation at all stages of a criminal case. If someone cannot afford a private attorney, the court will appoint a public defender to ensure that they have legal counsel. Arrested individuals are informed of this right, and any statement made without a lawyer present could be inadmissible in court.

**Foreign nationals arrested in Puerto Rico have the same rights as U.S. citizens when it comes to legal counsel, including the right to be informed of the charges and to consult with an attorney.** Foreign nationals should be aware that they can contact their consulate or embassy for assistance. Diplomatic representatives can help ensure that the arrested individual is treated fairly and in accordance with international law. However, while consular support can be useful, it does not replace the right to an attorney, and consulates cannot directly intervene in the legal process, provide legal advice or represent U.S. citizens in court, serve as official interpreters or translators, nor can they pay your legal, medical, or other fees.

## Bail[24]

Puerto Rico, as a U.S. territory, follows the same legal system as the mainland United States, which includes a bail system for those arrested, which allows an arrested individual to be released from custody while awaiting trial, as long as they can provide the necessary collateral or pay the required amount. Bail is typically set by a judge based on the severity of the crime, the flight risk of the defendant, and other factors, such as the individual's criminal history and ties to the community.

When someone is arrested in Puerto Rico, a judge will typically hold a **bail hearing within 24 to 48 hours**, where they will determine whether the defendant is eligible for bail. In most cases, the judge will set an amount, which can vary greatly depending on the charge. For less serious offenses, bail may be set at a lower amount, and sometimes a "signature bond" (where the defendant promises to appear in court without paying money upfront) may be granted. For more serious offenses, such as violent crimes or drug trafficking, bail amounts can be much higher, and in some cases, bail may be denied altogether.

Defendants can pay bail using cash, property, or a bail bond service, where a bail bondsman will post bail in exchange for a fee (usually around 10 percent of the total bail amount). If the defendant does not appear in court, the bail can be forfeited, and a warrant for arrest may be issued.

**For foreign visitors**, the bail process works similarly to how it would for Puerto Rican residents, but there are a few additional considerations:

- **Immigration Status:** If the arrested foreign national does not have legal immigration status in Puerto Rico, they may face additional scrutiny during the bail process. Immigration authorities could

---

24  https://casetext.com/statute/laws-of-puerto-rico/title-thirty-four-appendix-rules-of-court/ii-rules-of-criminal-procedure/chapter-xv-general-provisions/rule-218-bail-and-conditions-when-required-criteria-for-setting-review-of-amount-or-conditions-in-general

become involved, and in some cases, the individual may face deportation rather than being granted bail.

- **Bonding Companies:** Foreign visitors may find it more difficult to find a bonding company that will work with them, as many bail bond services require collateral or a local guarantor. This can be particularly challenging if the visitor does not have significant ties to Puerto Rico.

- **Passport or Consular Assistance:** Foreign nationals should contact their embassy or consulate as soon as possible after an arrest. In some cases, embassies can assist in securing bail or provide additional support during the legal process.

## Complaints Against Police

The Puerto Rico Police Department (PRPD) has faced significant scrutiny and criticism over the years. While many officers perform their duties with professionalism and dedication, **the overall reputation of the force has been tarnished by issues such as corruption, misconduct, and allegations of excessive force.** The PRPD has struggled with low public trust due to its history of **systemic issues,** including **allegations of police brutality,** especially in marginalized communities. The police have also been criticized for their **handling of sensitive cases like domestic violence and sexual assault,** often leading to victim-blaming or underreporting of crimes.

Despite these challenges, efforts have been made to reform the police force, including training initiatives, increased oversight, and attempts to address corruption. However, public perception remains mixed, and certain segments of the population, particularly those from low-income or rural areas, continue to express a lack of confidence in the police.

You can **file a complaint against a police officer** in Puerto Rico by contacting the **Office of Professional Responsibility** within the Puerto Rico Police Department (PRPD), either in person at a police station or by submitting a written complaint with detailed information about the incident, including date, location, and officer details. You can also reach out to the **Office of Legal Affairs** for further guidance.

## General Questions

1. *If I am convicted in Puerto Rico, am I likely to be released on bail pending the outcome of my appeal?* In Puerto Rico, whether you are granted bail after a conviction depends on the seriousness of the crime and other case specifics. For severe offenses like murder or sexual assault, bail is less likely to be granted during the appeal process. For less serious crimes, bail may be possible, especially if the defendant poses minimal risk of flight or danger. The decision is ultimately up to the judge, who will consider factors like the likelihood of success on appeal and the nature of the crime.

2. *What influences a bail determination?* Several factors influence bail decisions in Puerto Rico, including the **severity of the charge, the risk of flight, the threat to public safety, and the defendant's criminal history.** A judge will also consider the defendant's ties to the community and whether they might reoffend. The ability to pay bail can also play a role, as a defendant who cannot afford the set amount may remain in custody. The judge's goal is to ensure the defendant attends trial while balancing public safety concerns.

3. *Who is entitled to bail?* In Puerto Rico, most individuals arrested for a crime are entitled to bail unless they are charged with a serious offense like murder, sexual assault, or cases where the defendant is considered a flight risk or a danger to the community. Bail is not automatic and can be denied based on the nature of the crime, the defendant's criminal history, or the risk of reoffending. Ultimately, it's up to the judge to decide whether bail is appropriate based on the specific circumstances of the case.

4. *If I am arrested, how soon will I see a judge or magistrate?*
   After an arrest in Puerto Rico, you must be brought before a
   judge or magistrate **within 48 hours.** This initial appearance,
   known as an "arraignment," allows the judge to inform you of the
   charges, review the conditions of your detention, and determine
   whether bail will be granted. If you're unable to make bail, the
   judge will schedule your preliminary hearings and further legal
   proceedings.

5. *Will I be able to contact my country's embassy in Puerto Rico?*
   **Yes.** If you are a foreign national arrested in Puerto Rico, you are
   entitled to contact your embassy or consulate. **Under international law, you have the right to consular notification and assistance.** This allows your embassy to provide support, help you
   understand your rights, and assist in finding legal representation.
   It is important to inform authorities that you wish to contact
   your embassy as soon as possible after your arrest.

# JAILS VS. PRISONS: CONDITIONS & CULTURE

# JAILS VS. PRISONS: CONDITIONS & CULTURE

## Overview[25]

Puerto Rico's prison system consists of several detention facilities, including local jails and high-security prisons, which are operated by the **Puerto Rico Department of Corrections and Rehabilitation** (DCR). The DCR manages the system, which includes both male and female inmates, and is responsible for overseeing the conditions, security, and rehabilitation programs in the facilities.

Puerto Rico's prison system operates under both local law and federal guidelines. The primary goal is to house individuals who have been convicted of crimes, from minor offenses to serious felonies like murder or drug trafficking. Inmates in Puerto Rico are held in various levels of security, depending on the severity of their crimes and the perceived threat they pose.

**Jails** are typically used for individuals awaiting trial or those convicted of less severe crimes, while **prisons** house individuals convicted of more serious offenses. Some of the major prisons in Puerto Rico include the **Bayamón Prison**, **Ponce Correctional Complex**, and **Guayanilla Prison**, with several others scattered throughout the island.

---

25 https://www.prisonstudies.org/country/puerto-rico-usa

One of the most significant challenges facing Puerto Rico's prisons is **overcrowding**. With an estimated capacity of around 10,000 inmates, Puerto Rico's correctional facilities frequently exceed their capacity. This results in poor living conditions, increased tension among inmates, and difficulty in providing adequate healthcare, security, and rehabilitation programs.

Many prisons in Puerto Rico suffer from **poor infrastructure, insufficient resources**, and **lack of basic amenities.** This includes inadequate sanitation, limited access to educational or vocational training programs, and overcrowded cells. The conditions can lead to high levels of violence among inmates and against staff.

**Violence**, including gang-related activity, is prevalent in Puerto Rico's prisons. Gangs often control parts of the prison, including contraband distribution and the enforcement of informal rules. This creates a dangerous environment for both inmates and prison staff, with incidents of physical altercations and assaults being common.

**Access to adequate healthcare** is another challenge. Prisons in Puerto Rico struggle with providing proper medical care, including mental health services. Inmates with chronic conditions or mental health issues often face long wait times for treatment, which can worsen their conditions. This issue is exacerbated by the limited number of qualified healthcare providers in the system.

**Rehabilitation efforts** in Puerto Rico's prisons have often been underfunded and insufficient. While there are some programs aimed at reducing recidivism, such as education and vocational training, they are not widely available to all inmates. The lack of effective rehabilitation programs limits the chances for inmates to reintegrate into society successfully upon release.

Over the years, there have been various efforts to reform the prison system in Puerto Rico. These include attempts to improve conditions through infrastructure upgrades, the introduction of alternative sentencing for nonviolent offenders, and increased focus on rehabilitation. However, these efforts have often been hampered by budget constraints, political challenges, and the sheer scale of the issues within the system. In

2018, the Puerto Rican government entered into a consent decree with the U.S. Department of Justice, aiming to improve conditions in Puerto Rico's prisons. This decree mandated reforms regarding overcrowding, the use of excessive force by guards, and overall inmate treatment. The island also receives federal funding to help support its correctional system, but challenges remain in ensuring lasting change.

## Prison Conditions and Living Environment

Puerto Rico's prison system is divided into several housing units that correspond to **varying levels of security**, based on the severity of the inmates' crimes and their behavior.

**Maximum-security facilities** house the most dangerous and violent offenders. Inmates are typically confined to individual cells, and movement within the facility is tightly controlled. High-security prisons, such as the **Bayamón Prison**, are heavily guarded with restricted access to avoid escape or violent incidents. In **medium-security prisons** inmates have more privileges, including work-release programs and better access to rehabilitation programs. While the threat of violence still exists, it is less frequent than in high-security units. Finally, **minimum-security units** are typically for inmates with shorter sentences or non-violent crimes. Inmates may have more freedoms, such as more visitation opportunities and access to vocational training or educational programs. However, the overcrowded nature of Puerto Rico's prisons often blurs these distinctions, with many facilities operating at or above their capacity. This leads to tensions and a lack of adequate supervision in some units.

Living conditions in Puerto Rico's prisons can be harsh, and basic needs such as food, sanitation, and hygiene are often insufficient. The quality of **food** in Puerto Rico's prisons is another area of concern. Meals are typically simple and nutritionally inadequate, which can contribute to poor health outcomes for inmates. While prisoners are provided with three meals a day, the food often consists of cheap, processed items that lack variety and sufficient nutritional value.

Inmates report **poor sanitation and hygiene conditions** in many facilities. Overcrowding exacerbates the problem, with insufficient access to clean water and proper bathroom facilities. Dirty cells, clogged plumbing, and unsanitary conditions in common areas are common complaints. In some facilities, inmates have to share small spaces with little to no personal privacy. In addition to food and sanitation, many prisoners lack access to basic personal hygiene products such as soap, toothpaste, and toilet paper. In some cases, prisoners must rely on family members or friends to provide them with necessities. While the prison system provides minimal hygiene products, they are often not enough to meet inmates' needs, particularly in overcrowded settings.

Particularly problematic is **access to healthcare** in Puerto Rico's prisons. Inmates are entitled to basic healthcare services, but there are significant challenges in providing adequate treatment. While prisoners have access to general medical care, limited resources often result in long wait times for non-urgent treatments. There are reports of prisoners waiting weeks or even months for medical attention, especially for chronic illnesses. **Mental health care** is another area of concern. While some facilities have mental health professionals on staff, there are not enough to meet the demand, and those who do receive care often experience delays. **Puerto Rico has one of the highest suicide rates in U.S. prisons, partly due to a lack of proper mental health resources and care.**

For inmates requiring specialized treatments, such as surgery or long-term care for serious health conditions, access to care is limited. Some prisoners may need to be transported to outside medical facilities, but this can take time and resources, contributing to delays in treatment. In general, prison healthcare in Puerto Rico is underfunded and inadequate, with inmates often receiving care only when absolutely necessary, and only a small fraction getting comprehensive treatment for chronic or serious conditions.

## Inmate Rights and Legal Protections

Prisoners in Puerto Rico, like those in the U.S. mainland, retain **certain basic constitutional rights** under the **U.S. Constitution.** These rights are designed to ensure humane treatment and fair access to justice, although some rights are limited due to the nature of imprisonment.

Under the **Eighth Amendment** of the U.S. Constitution, inmates are protected from **cruel and unusual punishment**. This includes prohibitions on inhumane conditions such as overcrowding, inadequate medical care, and excessive use of force by prison staff. Prisoners are also entitled to **due process** under the **Fifth and Fourteenth Amendments**, which guarantee fair legal proceedings before being deprived of liberty. This includes the right to notice of charges, a fair hearing, and the ability to contest disciplinary actions within the prison system. Inmates retain the **right to free speech** and the **free exercise of religion**, though these rights can be restricted for safety and security reasons. For example, prisoners can practice their religion and request religious accommodations, but they may be limited in how they can communicate with the outside world, especially through mail or public demonstrations.

Inmates have the **right to access legal resources** and **file appeals**, including challenging their conviction or prison conditions. However, practical access to these resources can be difficult due to overcrowded facilities and limited support services. Inmates are entitled to law libraries and legal materials to help with their cases, but many face obstacles in fully utilizing these resources. While prisoners have the right to appeal their convictions or sentences, the process can be slow due to backlogs, and many rely on public defenders or legal aid organizations, which are often under-resourced. In some cases, inmates may experience delays in reaching external legal help, and accessing justice can be hindered by logistical barriers within the system.

**Abuse** within the prison system is a **significant concern** in Puerto Rico, as it is in many correctional systems worldwide. These violations can occur at the hands of both fellow prisoners and correctional staff. Inmates have **legal recourse through complaints** to the prison administration, as well as external human rights organizations, but access to effective remedies is limited by systemic issues like overcrowding and understaffing. Legal actions against abuse may be pursued through lawsuits or appeals, but victims often face significant challenges in proving their cases or securing accountability, due to the lack of resources, delays, and insufficient legal assistance.

## General Questions

1. *What is the difference between a jail and prison in Puerto Rico?* In Puerto Rico, as in most legal systems, jails and prisons serve distinct purposes. **Jails** are typically short-term detention facilities where individuals are held while awaiting trial or serving brief sentences (usually less than a year). They are operated by local law enforcement, such as municipal or county authorities. **Prisons**, on the other hand, are long-term correctional facilities for individuals who have been convicted of serious crimes and sentenced to longer terms (over a year). Prisons in Puerto Rico are managed by the Puerto Rico Department of Corrections and Rehabilitation and are generally larger, more secure institutions with various levels of security.

2. *Do jails and prisons offer religious services to inmates?* **Yes.** Both jails and prisons in Puerto Rico provide religious services to inmates. Religious activities and services are part of the rehabilitative programs offered to incarcerated individuals. Religious freedom is constitutionally protected, so inmates have the right to practice their faith while incarcerated. However, access to such services may vary depending on the facility and available resources.

3. *How do prisoners spend their time?* In Puerto Rico's prisons, inmates spend their time divided between daily routines and structured activities. Their time typically includes work assignments, participation in educational or vocational programs, recreation, religious services, and time for personal visits. Prisoners often have scheduled periods for physical exercise, which may include outdoor or indoor sports activities. Those involved in educational programs can attend classes aimed at completing high school or pursuing higher education, while vocational training allows prisoners to learn skills like carpentry, plumbing, or computer skills. Prisoners also have time for personal reflection or to engage in other rehabilitative activities, such as therapy or

counseling sessions. However, the availability of these programs varies depending on the security level and the resources of the facility.

4. *What type of jobs can inmates perform?* Inmates in Puerto Rico's correctional facilities are required to work, typically in jobs that help maintain the prison and contribute to its operations. These jobs may include tasks such as kitchen work, janitorial duties, laundry, maintenance, and groundskeeping. Some inmates may also be assigned to more specialized tasks like working in a prison's factory and producing furniture, textiles, or other goods. Additionally, vocational programs often allow inmates to learn trades like carpentry, electrical work, or welding, which they can then use to work in prison-based workshops or in jobs after their release. Some prisoners may also work in jobs that assist with the rehabilitation process, such as serving as peer mentors, tutors for educational programs, or in administrative roles within the facility.

5. *How does the prison commissary system work in Puerto Rico?* In Puerto Rico's prisons, the commissary system allows inmates to purchase various goods and personal items that are not provided by the facility. Items available at the commissary typically include snacks, hygiene products, writing materials, clothing, over-the-counter medications, and sometimes electronics like radios or headphones, depending on the security level of the prison. Inmates can purchase these items using funds from their personal accounts, which are often supplemented by family or friends who send money. However, the prices of commissary items can be higher than typical retail prices. The system is intended to give prisoners a degree of personal autonomy and comfort, but it can also lead to tension or inequality between inmates who have more or less financial support from the outside.

6. *What type of medical care do prisoners receive?* Inmates in Puerto Rico's correctional facilities are entitled to basic medical care, which includes access to healthcare services such as general medical exams, treatment for illnesses, dental care, and mental health services. However, the healthcare system faces challenges such as overcrowding and limited resources, leading to delays and sometimes substandard care. For severe cases, inmates may be transferred to outside hospitals. Mental health services are available but often understaffed, resulting in insufficient attention to psychiatric needs.

7. *What is prison culture in Puerto Rico?* Prison culture in Puerto Rico, like in many correctional facilities, is shaped by factors such as security level, inmate population, and the socio-political environment. The culture can be tough, with strong solidarity among inmates based on neighborhood, social class, or gang affiliation. A hierarchical structure exists, where older or more powerful inmates often hold authority, leading to violence and intimidation. The code of conduct emphasizes respect, survival, and personal boundaries, resulting in alliances or conflicts. While inmates form bonds through activities like religious services or sports, these can also fuel power struggles. Overcrowding and limited resources contribute to frequent violence and psychological stress.

CHAPTER 12

# HELPING A FRIEND OR RELATIVE IMPRISONED IN PUERTO RICO

**IN THIS CHAPTER**

- Overview
- Sending Food, Supplies, and Money to an Inmate
- Mail, Phone Calls, and Visitation
- Prison Scams
- Upon Release

# HELPING A FRIEND OR RELATIVE IMPRISONED IN PUERTO RICO

## Overview

If a friend or relative is imprisoned in Puerto Rico, the first step is to **contact local authorities**, such as the **Puerto Rico Police Department** or the **correctional facility**, to confirm their whereabouts and gather information. You should then **reach out to your country's embassy or consulate** in Puerto Rico for assistance. The embassy can help by providing legal resources, arranging communication with local attorneys, and ensuring that the detainee's basic rights are respected. For U.S. citizens, the embassy in San Juan can notify family members, monitor the detainee's treatment, and help facilitate consular visits. While the embassy cannot provide direct legal representation, it can offer support by guiding you to English-speaking attorneys who specialize in Puerto Rican law.

When dealing with an arrest in Puerto Rico, it's important to remember that while Puerto Rico is a U.S. territory and follows U.S. federal law, it also has its own local legal system. This means there may be **specific laws and procedures unique to Puerto Rico** that could differ from those on the U.S. mainland. If your relative or friend is incarcerated, understanding local conditions and knowing what resources are available for inmates is essential.

Additionally, the legal system in Puerto Rico operates in both Spanish and English, but many legal proceedings and documents are in Spanish, so it may be helpful to work with a bilingual attorney or legal translator if you're not fluent in the language. Finally, Puerto Rico's culture and social norms might affect how detainees are treated. For instance, the prison system is known for having strong internal codes of conduct among inmates, and outside help from family members or legal representatives can sometimes play a key role in ensuring fair treatment. You should be prepared to advocate for your relative or friend with local authorities and legal professionals who understand the local dynamics.

## Sending Food, Supplies, and Money to an Inmate

In Puerto Rico, as in many places, the rules regarding sending food and supplies to inmates vary depending on the correctional facility and its specific regulations. Generally, family and friends are not allowed to bring food directly to an inmate in prison or jail due to security concerns and to maintain control over what inmates consume.

Family members and friends can send money to inmates through commissary accounts, which inmates use to purchase snacks, hygiene products, and other personal items. This can typically be done via electronic transfer services or through money orders, depending on the facility's procedures.

As for **food**, most correctional institutions provide three meals a day to inmates, though the quality and quantity of food can vary. Inmates can sometimes receive food packages, but these **are subject to approval and must adhere to facility guidelines**. Certain items, such as perishable goods or food that could pose a security risk, are usually prohibited. Non-perishable items like packaged snacks, canned goods, or other sealed items may be allowed, but it is important to check the specific rules of the facility.

In some cases, inmates can **receive care packages** with toiletries, clothing, or other necessities. However, these packages typically must be sent through approved vendors or services rather than directly from family members, and they are subject to inspection.

**It's crucial to consult with the specific jail or prison to understand their exact regulations for sending food or supplies, as policies can differ between institutions in Puerto Rico.**

## Mail, Phone Calls, and Visitation

*Phone Calls*

In Puerto Rican prisons, inmates are **not permitted to have cell phones** due to security concerns. Instead, they are given access to **prison-operated phones** to make calls. These calls are typically **collect calls** or paid through a pre-funded account, which can be set up by the inmate or their family. However, inmates **cannot receive incoming calls**, except in rare emergency situations.

Phone access is often limited and can vary depending on the specific prison. Inmates generally have designated times to use the phone, and these calls are **monitored and recorded** to ensure safety and prevent illegal activities. The length and frequency of calls are also regulated, with good behavior sometimes earning inmates additional privileges, such as longer or more frequent phone calls.

*Visitation*

Visiting someone in prison in Puerto Rico involves several important rules and procedures, all aimed at ensuring security and maintaining order. Inmates are **generally allowed visits from family members, close friends, and legal representatives**, although visitors **must first be approved by the facility**. To be added to an inmate's approved visitation list, visitors typically need to submit their details in advance. Attorneys and legal representatives, however, are granted visits without such approval, as long as they comply with the facility's security measures.

The frequency of visits varies, with most inmates allowed **one or two visits per week**, though additional visits may be granted based on the inmate's behavior or special circumstances. Some facilities offer extended visitations during holidays or for inmates with particular needs, such as medical or emotional support. **Visitors should check the specific facility for detailed information on visiting hours, as these can vary widely.**

When visiting, there are several things to keep in mind. All visitors must present valid government-issued identification, like a passport or driver's license, to gain entry. A strict dress code is enforced, prohibiting revealing attire or clothing deemed inappropriate for a correctional environment. Visitors are also subject to security checks, including metal detectors, bag searches, and even pat downs. Any form of contraband, such as drugs, weapons, or unauthorized electronics, is strictly prohibited.

**Visit durations** are usually limited, typically ranging **from 30 minutes to an hour**, but may be extended in special circumstances. Children are allowed to visit but must be accompanied by an adult, and facilities often limit the number of minors allowed at one time. While most communication is in Spanish, non-Spanish-speaking visitors might need a translator, especially in rural areas.

Some prisons in Puerto Rico also offer **video visitation** as a modern alternative to in-person visits, especially for families who may not be able to travel long distances. However, as with in-person visits, video sessions are subject to security protocols, and visitation privileges can be revoked for inmates who engage in disruptive behavior. **For the most accurate and up-to-date information, visitors should always contact the facility directly before planning their visit.**

## Prison Scams

Prison **scams targeting families of incarcerated individuals** in Puerto Rico are unfortunately common and can be both emotionally and financially damaging. Scammers often exploit the stress and urgency that family members feel when their loved ones are in prison, manipulating them into sending money under false pretenses. These scams typically involve someone posing as a prison official, a lawyer, or even the inmate themselves, claiming the person in custody needs immediate financial help for medical emergencies, legal fees, or even to settle disputes within the prison.

One prevalent scam is the **"collect call scam,"** where the fraudster impersonates the inmate, convincing family members that they are in danger and need money. The scammer might ask for money to resolve a supposed emergency, further pressuring the family to send funds quickly. In another version, scammers may call **pretending to be representatives from a legal firm or charitable organization**, asking for donations for inmates' medical needs, educational programs, or prison improvements. These claims are often entirely fabricated.

To avoid falling victim, it's crucial to be cautious when someone pressures you for money, especially when they demand wire transfers, prepaid gift cards, or other untraceable payment methods. These are typical signs of a scam. If you suspect you're being scammed, immediately **stop communication and verify the situation directly with the prison**. Always use official contact information from the facility, not what the scammer provides.

If you've already sent money and believe you've been scammed, it's essential to **document all interactions and report the incident to the local authorities**. In Puerto Rico, you can contact the Puerto Rico Police Department or the Department of Justice for assistance. **Foreign nationals should also contact their embassy or consulate** for guidance on how to proceed with the report and safeguard their interests.

**Raising awareness is key**. Ensuring that others know about these types of scams can prevent further victims. Family and friends should be informed about how to handle urgent requests and how to confirm the legitimacy of any communication regarding their incarcerated loved ones.

## Upon Release

Upon release from prison or jail in Puerto Rico, foreign nationals are generally subject to the same rules and procedures as local residents, but there are a few additional considerations to keep in mind.

Foreigners who have been incarcerated in Puerto Rico may face **immigration-related consequences** upon release, depending on the nature of their offense and their immigration status. If the individual is in the U.S. illegally or violated U.S. immigration laws, they could be subject to **deportation** proceedings once they complete their sentence. In some cases, they may be detained by **U.S. Immigration and Customs Enforcement (ICE)** or the **Puerto Rican authorities** until deportation can be arranged.

In addition, after release, there could be **restrictions on certain activities**, such as leaving the island or entering specific areas, particularly if the individual is on probation or has conditions attached to their release. For example, individuals **on probation** may be required to check in with their probation officer regularly, attend rehabilitation programs, or comply with other conditions set by the court.

Foreign nationals may also be required to **report to immigration authorities** if they are not U.S. citizens, which could influence their ability to stay or work in Puerto Rico or the mainland U.S. Any failure to comply with these post-release obligations could result in further legal consequences, including the possibility of re-incarceration or deportation.

# THE ADMINISTRATION OF JUSTICE

CHAPTER 13

# THE ADMINISTRATION
# OF JUSTICE

## Puerto Rico's Legal System

Puerto Rico's legal system is rooted in a combination of **Spanish civil law** and **American common law**, shaped by its unique status as a U.S. territory. Originally, Puerto Rico operated under **Spanish colonial law**, which was largely based on the **Napoleonic Code** and the **Spanish Civil Code**. These legal principles governed Puerto Rican society for centuries, shaping everything from property rights to criminal laws. However, when Puerto Rico became a U.S. territory in 1898 following the Spanish-American War, the island's legal system began to evolve to incorporate aspects of U.S. law. The **Jones-Shafroth Act of 1917**, which granted U.S. citizenship to Puerto Ricans, established a framework for Puerto Rico's legal system under American rule. This was followed by the **Puerto Rican Constitution of 1952**, which created the Commonwealth of Puerto Rico and allowed the island to govern itself under a form of **limited sovereignty** while remaining a U.S. territory. Today, Puerto Rico follows a **dual legal system**, integrating both civil law traditions inherited from Spain and elements of U.S. constitutional law.[26]

---

26  https://www.nyulawglobal.org/globalex/puerto_rico.html

*Key components of Puerto Rico's Legal System*

The **Constitution of Puerto Rico**, adopted in 1952, serves as the island's supreme law, outlining fundamental individual rights, the separation of powers, and the structure of government. It guarantees civil rights and liberties while establishing the framework for legislative processes.

Puerto Rico's **judiciary** consists of three levels: the **Supreme Court**, **Court of Appeals**, and **Court of First Instance**. The Supreme Court is the highest legal authority, interpreting the constitution and addressing key legal matters. The Court of Appeals acts as the intermediate appellate court, while the Court of First Instance handles initial trials and other judicial proceedings.[27]

The **legislative branch** is bicameral, composed of the **Senate** (27 members) and the **House of Representatives** (51 members), with both serving four-year terms. This structure reflects Puerto Rico's representative democracy, similar to U.S. state legislatures.[28]

The **executive branch** is led by an elected **governor**, who serves a four-year term. The governor is responsible for implementing laws, managing government functions, and exercising veto power over legislation. The executive branch also includes various departments managing areas such as education, health, and public safety.[29]

Puerto Rico has a **dual legal system** combining **civil law** (influenced by Spanish traditions) and **common law** (influenced by U.S. law), particularly in private law matters. This requires courts to balance and resolve conflicts between civil codes and American legal principles.[30]

---

27  https://www.nyulawglobal.org/globalex/puerto_rico.html

28  https://law-miami.libguides.com/PuertoRicoLegalResearch

29  https://blogs.loc.gov/law/2022/11/
the-commonwealth-of-puerto-rico-and-its-government-structure

30  https://chambers.com/content/item/3503

As an **unincorporated U.S. territory, U.S. federal law** applies in many areas, such as **immigration, bankruptcy,** and **intellectual property law.** However, Puerto Rico has **local autonomy** over many other areas, particularly those relating to family law, property, and education. This unique relationship can sometimes cause legal conflicts or ambiguities, particularly in areas like **taxation** and **voting rights.**

## The Judiciary

The judiciary in Puerto Rico is structured similarly to the U.S. federal system but adapted to local legal needs. It operates under the framework established by the Constitution of Puerto Rico, which ensures an independent judiciary. Puerto Rico's judicial system consists of three main tiers: the Supreme Court, the Court of Appeals, and the Court of First Instance. Each level serves a specific purpose within the legal framework, allowing for both initial adjudication of cases and appellate review of lower court decisions:

1. **Supreme Court of Puerto Rico:** The highest court in the judicial system, the **Supreme Court** is the ultimate authority on legal matters. It has the power to review decisions made by lower courts and has the final say on constitutional issues. The court is composed of a Chief Justice and several Associate Justices, who are appointed by the Governor and confirmed by the Senate. The Supreme Court's rulings are binding across Puerto Rico, and it plays a key role in interpreting the Puerto Rican Constitution and resolving disputes between governmental entities.[31]

2. **Court of Appeals:** This is the **intermediate appellate court** in Puerto Rico. It hears appeals from the **Court of First Instance** and other lower courts. The Court of Appeals has the authority to review the application of law in previous cases and to correct errors made by trial judges. It consists of multiple panels of judges, each tasked with evaluating cases on appeal. The decisions made by the Court of Appeals are typically final, though certain matters can be brought

---

31  https://poderjudicial.pr/eng/supreme-court/

before the Supreme Court if they involve significant legal questions or constitutional issues.[32]

3. **Court of First Instance:** This is the **trial court** where most legal cases begin. It handles both **civil** and **criminal cases**, including family law, commercial disputes, and personal injury cases. The Court of First Instance is divided into various branches, including specialized divisions like **Family Courts, Probate Courts**, and **Criminal Courts**. The judges here are tasked with determining the facts of each case and issuing rulings based on the evidence presented.[33]

As mentioned above, Puerto Rico's judiciary is unique due to its **mixed legal system**, combining **civil law** (influenced by Spain) and **common law** (from the U.S.). This creates a complex legal environment, particularly in areas like private law. The judiciary operates with **judicial independence**, ensuring decisions are made without political interference. While **Spanish** is the primary language used in courts, **English** is also employed, especially in federal matters.

The judiciary system in Puerto Rico faces numerous challenges that hinder its effectiveness and accessibility. A significant issue is the ongoing **financial and resource constraints**, which have led to budget cuts affecting the operational capabilities of the courts and legal services. Additionally, an estimated 75 percent of litigation parties **lack legal representation**, often due to economic barriers and insufficient funding for legal aid programs. **Language barriers** further complicate legal proceedings, as a substantial portion of the population is not fully fluent in English, impacting their ability to navigate the judicial process effectively. The **complexity of Puerto Rico's unique legal framework**— characterized by its mixed legal traditions—adds another layer of challenges, requiring judges and legal practitioners to reconcile conflicting legal principles from civil and common law. Combined, these factors

---

32  https://law-miami.libguides.com/PuertoRicoLegalResearch

33  https://poderjudicial.pr/eng/community-education/legal-topics/ government-and-court-system/court-system/

contribute to a systemic issue that threatens the integrity and fairness of the judiciary.[34]

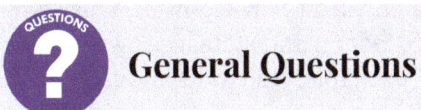 **General Questions**

1. *Will the court treat first-time offenders and tourists with more leniency?* While the court may consider a defendant's criminal history, including whether they are a first-time offender, the treatment of first-time offenders or tourists will generally **depend on the severity of the crime**. In Puerto Rico, as with many jurisdictions, the severity of the offense, the circumstances, and whether it's a misdemeanor or felony typically influence sentencing. However, tourists may face additional challenges, such as language barriers or unfamiliarity with local laws, but their status as a foreigner doesn't automatically guarantee leniency. In some cases, tourists may receive harsher treatment if the crime is seen as disrupting the tourism industry or violating local customs.

2. *If I am charged with a crime, which court is likely to hear my case?* The court that will hear your case in Puerto Rico depends on the severity of the charge. For most criminal offenses, the **Court of First Instance** (*Tribunal de Primera Instancia*) will initially handle the case. This court has jurisdiction over both felony and misdemeanor cases. If your case involves a serious offense, such as a felony, it could be transferred to the **Superior Court**, which deals with more severe crimes. The **Court of Appeals** would hear any appeals if you are convicted, and in rare cases, the **Supreme Court of Puerto Rico** could get involved for constitutional matters or significant legal issues.

---

34 https://derecho.uprrp.edu/revistajuridica/wp-content/uploads/ sites/4/2017/07/03.-Acces-to-Justice-in-Puerto-Rico_Rhode-Hernandez-86REVJURUPR818.pdf

3. *What is the standard of proof in a criminal case in Puerto Rico?* In Puerto Rico, the standard of proof in criminal cases is **"beyond a reasonable doubt."** This is the highest standard in the legal system and requires that the prosecution prove the defendant's guilt to such an extent that no reasonable doubt remains in the minds of the jury or judge. If the prosecution fails to meet this standard, the defendant is entitled to an acquittal. This standard is consistent with the U.S. federal and state legal systems, as Puerto Rico follows U.S. legal principles due to its status as a U.S. territory.

 ## Law of the Land True Story

In *United States v. Vaello-Madero* (2022), the Supreme Court ruled 8-1 that Congress has the authority to exclude Puerto Rico residents from receiving Supplemental Security Income (SSI) benefits. The case arose when José Luis Vaello-Madero, who had received SSI benefits while living in New York, moved to Puerto Rico and continued receiving payments until 2016. The federal government sued Vaello-Madero for US$28,081 in overpaid benefits. Vaello-Madero argued that excluding Puerto Rican residents from SSI violated his constitutional right to equal protection. The Court, in an opinion written by Justice Brett Kavanaugh, upheld the exclusion, citing the Constitution's text, historical practices, and legal precedents.

The ruling brings attention to the constitutional tensions between federal law and Puerto Rico's local legal framework, revealing the complexities of the territory's relationship with U.S. law and the ongoing debate about Puerto Rico's political status. The case highlights how the dual legal systems—federal versus local—can create disparities in rights and protections for Puerto Rican residents.

## Takeaways

- Puerto Rico's legal system is a hybrid, blending **Spanish civil law** with **American common law** due to its unique status as a U.S. territory. This combination creates a complex legal environment where courts must navigate both civil codes and U.S. legal principles.

- Puerto Rico's judiciary follows a three-tiered structure, consisting of the **Supreme Court**, the **Court of Appeals**, and the **Court of First Instance**. The Supreme Court is the highest authority, interpreting constitutional issues and providing binding rulings across the territory.

- The judiciary in Puerto Rico faces significant **resource constraints**, with **budget cuts** affecting the operational efficiency of the courts. Additionally, **language barriers** and a high rate of **self-representation** (due to economic factors) further complicate the judicial process.

- The legal tension between **U.S. federal law** and **Puerto Rico's local law** often results in conflicts, particularly in areas like taxation and federal benefits.

- The legal process in Puerto Rico is similar to the U.S. system, particularly in criminal cases, where the **standard of proof** is "beyond a reasonable doubt." This aligns with U.S. legal principles and is crucial for ensuring fair trials.

# CRIME VICTIM ASSISTANCE

# CRIME VICTIM ASSISTANCE

## Overview

In Puerto Rico, crime victims have access to a range of services to help them recover from the trauma of crime, seek justice, and rebuild their lives. These services include legal aid, psychological counseling, financial compensation, and protection from further harm. Victims of crimes such as domestic violence, sexual assault, human trafficking, and violent crimes are among those who can benefit from victim assistance programs.

Financial support primarily comes from the Crime Victims Compensation Program, which provides reimbursement for expenses incurred due to violent crimes. This can include medical bills, funeral expenses, counseling, and lost wages.[35] On the non-financial side, programs offer crisis intervention, counseling, legal aid, and emotional support to help victims cope with their experiences.[36] These resources aim to address not just the immediate needs of victims but also assist in their long-term recovery and reintegration into society. For example, Puerto Rico Victim Assistance Program (*Programa de Ayuda a Víctimas del Delito*) provides mental health services, including counseling and therapy, for victims of violence and crime. Specialized services are available for those affected

---

35 https://www.safeta.org/page/prpayment/

36 https://vawnet.org/material/
victims-crime-act-voca-victim-assistance-formula-grant-program

by domestic violence, sexual assault, and other traumatic events. The Department of Health offers free or low-cost psychological support for crime victims through clinics and outreach programs.

The government plays a critical role in the provision of victim assistance through a variety of programs funded by the Victims of Crime Act (VOCA)[37]. These programs are designed to support local agencies and organizations that assist victims of crime across the nation, including Puerto Rico. For instance, the Puerto Rico Department of Justice oversees the Crime Victims Compensation Office, which manages claims for financial aid stemming from incidents of violent crime. Through these government initiatives, victims can access essential services and advocacy to ensure their rights are upheld throughout the criminal justice process.[38] Moreover, the Department of Justice has implemented the "Bill of Rights of the Victims and Witnesses of Crimes," which guarantees victims certain rights, such as the right to be treated with fairness and respect, and the right to receive timely notifications about criminal proceedings.[39]

In addition to government resources, a multitude of non-government organizations (NGOs) actively work in Puerto Rico to provide comprehensive support to crime victims. NGOs often fill gaps in government services, particularly concerning culturally sensitive and accessible care for diverse populations Organizations such as BastaYaPR, which advocates against violence, and the PR Health Justice Center, delivering clinical forensic services to survivors of sexual violence, are examples of the community-based efforts to assist victims.[40] These NGOs engage in direct service provision, including counseling, legal assistance, and support groups tailored to the unique needs of victims. Furthermore, many NGOs offer crisis hotline services and collaborate with local authorities to coordinate responses to domestic violence, sexual assault, and other serious offenses.

37  https://ovc.ojp.gov/states/puerto-rico

38  https://www.justice.gov/usao-pr/victim-witness-assistance

39  https://poderjudicial.pr/eng/community-education/legal-topics/
    criminal-cases/rights-of-victims-and-witnesses

40  https://www.justice.gov/usao-pr/victim-witness-assistance

Here are some Important Emergency Numbers in Puerto Rico:

- **Emergency Number (Police/Fire/Medical):** 911
- **Domestic Violence Hotline:** 1-800-981-0023
- **Puerto Rico Police Department (Policía de Puerto Rico):** 787-343-2020
- **Sexual Assault Support and Helpline:** 1-800-981-0023
- **Victim assistance program (Programa de Asistencia a las Víctimas del Delito):** 787-753-1256
- **Anti-trafficking Hotline:** 1-888-373-7888

## What to Do If You Are the Victim of a Crime

If you are the victim of a crime in Puerto Rico, the first thing to do is **ensure your immediate safety**. If you're in danger, leave the area and find a safe place, such as a friend's house or a public area. For emergencies, call 911 to reach police, medical help, or fire services.

Once safe, **report the crime** to the Puerto Rico Police Department by calling 787-343-2020 or again dialing 911. Provide as many details as possible, including the time, location, and description of the crime and the perpetrator. After the police arrive, get a copy of the **police report** (*Denuncia*), which will be crucial for future legal processes.

Next, **seek medical attention**, even if your injuries seem minor. Hospitals and urgent care centers will treat any wounds, document your injuries, and may collect important evidence, particularly if the crime involved assault or sexual violence. Preserving evidence is vital. Do not alter or clean any items related to the crime, such as clothing or belongings, as they could be key for the investigation. Take photographs of any visible injuries or damage to property, and keep a detailed record of the event, including dates, times, and descriptions of what happened.

Consider reaching out to **victim support services** for legal, emotional, and practical help. The **Puerto Rico Victim Assistance Program**

(787-753-1256) can guide you through the legal process, assist with compensation applications, and offer counseling. If you are dealing with domestic violence or harassment, organizations like the **National Domestic Violence Hotline** (1-800-981-0023) can connect you to safe shelters, legal services, and support networks. If you feel threatened or at risk of further harm, you may want to file for a **protection order** through the court system, which can prevent the perpetrator from contacting you. Also, look into applying for **financial assistance** through the **Puerto Rico Crime Victim Compensation Fund**, which can cover expenses related to medical bills, lost wages, and funeral costs.

Stay in contact with the police to follow the investigation, and keep all records and evidence related to the crime. Seek counseling and psychological support through organizations that offer trauma services, as coping with the aftermath of a crime can be difficult. Finally, **know your rights as a victim** under Puerto Rican law. You are entitled to be informed, protected, and treated with dignity throughout the process.

## Common Tourist Scams in Puerto Rico

In Puerto Rico, as with any popular tourist destination, tourists are generally more at risk of being targeted by scams rather than violent crimes. While violent crime can occur, especially in certain neighborhoods or under specific circumstances, **scams are more prevalent**, especially in tourist-heavy areas.

One of the most common scams involves **overcharging for taxis**. It's not unusual for some taxi drivers in tourist areas to either avoid using the meter or take longer routes to inflate the fare. To avoid this, always **agree on a fare** before getting in, or choose to use **ride-sharing apps** like Uber, which offer clear and fair pricing.

Another prevalent scam is the **timeshare or vacation club pitch**, where tourists are lured by promises of free gifts or discounted activities in exchange for attending high-pressure sales presentations. While the deals may seem tempting, they often end up being a scam. To protect yourself, it's best to **research** any offers before accepting and avoid falling for "too good to be true" offers. If you do end up attending a presentation and feel uncomfortable, it's perfectly okay to **walk away**.

**Street performers and vendors** are also common sources of scams. They might hand you a "free" gift, like flowers or bracelets, and then demand payment when you try to leave. The trick is to **politely decline any unsolicited gifts or offers**, especially from strangers on the street. If you find yourself in a situation where you've accepted something and are being pressured for money, **stay calm and firmly refuse to pay**. If necessary, walk away.

For those seeking excursions or tours, there are **fake tour operators** who offer deeply discounted prices for activities that either don't exist or are far below expectations. To avoid this, always book through **reputable companies** or get recommendations from trusted sources like your hotel. If you encounter a scam, and you've already made a payment, contact your **credit card company** to dispute the charges and report the incident to local authorities.

Another important tip is to **protect your personal information**. Avoid using unsecure ATMs and be cautious when entering your credit card information in tourist-heavy areas, where scammers sometimes use skimming devices. If you notice any suspicious activity on your bank or credit card statements, **report it immediately** to your bank or card provider. In case your wallet or phone is stolen, report it to the police and cancel your cards right away.

It's also essential to **trust your instincts**. If something feels off, it's okay to step back and reassess the situation. Always remain calm and walk away from situations that make you feel uncomfortable. If you do find yourself in trouble, **hotel staff** or **local authorities** can often offer guidance or assist in handling the situation.

Lastly, **keep your valuables secure** by storing important items like passports, money, and electronics in a safe place, whether it's a hotel safe or a secure bag designed to prevent theft. Stay mindful in crowded areas or when navigating through public spaces, as pickpocketing is another common issue in tourist spots.

## Sexual Assault

In the immediate aftermath of a sexual assault, it is essential for survivors to **prioritize their safety and health**. First, survivors should seek a safe place away from the perpetrator. If the situation allows, contacting friends, family, or a crisis hotline can provide immediate emotional support and guidance. Additionally, **accessing medical care is critical**. Survivors are encouraged to visit a hospital or clinic that specializes in forensic examinations. These facilities can provide important medical treatment, collect evidence, and prescribe medications to prevent sexually transmitted infections and unintended pregnancies.[41]

It is crucial to note that survivors are not required to report the assault to law enforcement to receive medical care or a forensic exam. They may choose to have a sexual assault forensic exam, commonly referred to as a "rape kit," performed without making a formal report. This allows for the collection of vital evidence that can be used if the survivor later decides to pursue legal action.

**Reporting a sexual assault** can be a daunting step for survivors, often fraught with fear and confusion. In Puerto Rico, survivors have multiple avenues for filing a report. The primary method is to **contact local law enforcement** by dialing 911 or going directly to a police station. Survivors can also seek assistance from **specialized units** within law enforcement that focus on sexual violence cases, which are typically staffed by officers trained to handle these sensitive matters.[42]

When filing a report, it is crucial to **document as much information as possible**, including details about the incident, any witnesses, and the perpetrator's description if known. Survivors may wish to bring a trusted family member, friend, or advocate for support during the process. Additionally, survivors should inquire about resources available for counseling and legal assistance, as many organizations can help navigate the legal system.

---

41  https://rainn.org/articles/steps-you-can-take-after-sexual-assault

42  https://www.nsvrc.org/states-territories/puerto-rico

In Puerto Rico, victims of sexual assault are entitled to several rights aimed at protecting them throughout the legal process. Under the *"Bill of Rights of the Victims and Witnesses of Crimes,"* survivors have the right to be treated with fairness, dignity, and respect. This legislation affords victims the right to receive timely notifications about their cases, including information regarding criminal proceedings and changes in the status of the perpetrator. Furthermore, victims have the right to access necessary medical and psychological services without delay.

It is also important for survivors to be aware of the legal protection measures available to them, such as restraining orders or protective orders, especially if they feel threatened by the perpetrator. Engaging with a legal advocate or counselor can provide essential guidance in understanding and exercising these rights effectively.

## Safety Recommendations

Preventing future assaults and enhancing personal safety is an important part of recovery for survivors. Here are several safety recommendations that can help individuals protect themselves:

- Stay vigilant in unfamiliar environments and avoid secluded areas, especially at night.
- Whenever possible, travel with friends and avoid being alone in potentially risky situations. Having a support network can provide both safety and emotional stability.
- If a situation or individual makes you uncomfortable, leave immediately. Your feelings are valid, and trusting your gut can be a crucial protective measure.
- Utilize apps that inform friends or family members of your whereabouts and share your live location if you feel threatened.
- Create a personalized safety plan outlining steps to take if feeling threatened, including numbers to call, places to go, and individuals to contact for help.[43]

---

43  https://police.charlotte.edu/safety/sexual-assault-prevention/
reduce-risk-becoming-sexual-assault-victim

## Consular Assistance[44]

The **U.S. embassy and consulate in Puerto Rico** provide **essential support to American citizens who become victims of crime abroad**. They assist with understanding legal rights, reporting crimes, and finding local legal representation. The consulate helps victims connect with local authorities, ensuring police reports are filed promptly. They also offer lists of local legal resources and provide referrals to lawyers specializing in criminal cases.

In addition to **legal aid**, the consulate offers **emotional support** and can direct victims to **mental health services**. They also facilitate **medical care** by connecting victims with hospitals or clinics for trauma-related treatment. If needed, the consulate can assist with **evacuation** and help victims communicate with family members for additional support.[45]

 **General Questions**

1. *If I am a victim of a crime, can I legally be compensated?*
   **Yes.** As a crime victim in Puerto Rico, you may be eligible for compensation through the Puerto Rico Crime Victim Compensation Fund, which is funded by the federal government and managed by local authorities. This fund can cover medical expenses, counseling, lost wages, and other financial losses incurred due to the crime. Additionally, there are Victims of Crime Act (VOCA) programs that offer financial assistance for crime-related expenses, and the Puerto Rico Victim Assistance Program can help guide you through the application process. You should

---

44  https://travel.state.gov/content/travel/en/international-travel/emergencies/crime.html

45  https://ovc.ojp.gov/sites/g/files/xyckuh226/files/publications/infores/ServingVictimsAbroad/firststeps.html

contact local authorities or victim advocacy groups for more
details on how to apply.

2. *If a family member falls victim to homicide, can I bring the
   body back to my home country?* **Yes.** If a family member dies in
   Puerto Rico, you can bring their body back to your home country, but this process involves specific steps. You will need to contact a funeral home in Puerto Rico that specializes in repatriation
   services. They will assist in handling all necessary paperwork, including obtaining the death certificate, complying with embassy
   or consular requirements, and arranging for the transportation of
   the body. Additionally, the U.S. embassy or consulate can provide
   assistance to ensure all legal and logistical matters are properly
   addressed.

3. *If a family member falls victim to homicide, will I receive any
   assistance from the Puerto Rican government?* **Yes.** If a family
   member is the victim of homicide in Puerto Rico, you may receive assistance from the Puerto Rican government through the
   Victim Assistance Program and other state-run resources. This
   can include emotional support, crisis counseling, and potentially financial aid for funeral expenses or other immediate needs.
   The Puerto Rico Department of Justice and other agencies may
   also offer legal and financial support, as well as grief counseling.
   It's recommended to contact the Puerto Rico Victim Assistance
   Program for guidance and to access the available services.

# POLICE

## IN THIS CHAPTER

- Overview
- Police Response
- Police and Community Relations
- Police Use of Force
- Law of the Land True Story

# POLICE

## Overview

The police force in Puerto Rico operates through a **multi-tiered structure** that includes **federal, state,** and **municipal agencies,** each with its own responsibilities in maintaining public safety and enforcing the law. At the **federal level,** agencies like **the FBI** and **the DEA** play crucial roles, especially in addressing federal crimes, drug trafficking, and terrorism. They work alongside local authorities but focus on matters that fall under federal jurisdiction.

The backbone of law enforcement in Puerto Rico is the **Puerto Rico Police Department** (PRPD), which is the **primary state law enforcement agency.** With approximately 12,000 officers, the PRPD is responsible for a wide range of duties, from general crime investigation and traffic enforcement to providing support to local municipal police. Its paramilitary structure includes various divisions dedicated to specific areas such as counterterrorism and special weapons teams.

Each of the 78 municipalities in Puerto Rico has its own **local police force,** which handles law enforcement within its jurisdiction. These municipal police departments deal with local issues like traffic violations and community engagement. In larger cities like San Juan, municipal police forces consist of several hundred officers, while smaller municipalities may have fewer than 50.

## Police Response

The Puerto Rico Police Department, the primary law enforcement agency, along with municipal police and federal agencies, work together to address crime and maintain order on the island. Their key functions include:

- **Crime Prevention and Law Enforcement:** The PRPD is responsible for preventing and responding to crimes ranging from petty offenses to serious criminal activities, including drug trafficking, gang violence, domestic violence, and organized crime. Municipal police handle local issues like traffic violations, noise complaints, and public disturbances, while also assisting in broader criminal investigations when necessary.

- **Emergency Response:** Police are the first responders to emergencies, including accidents, natural disasters, and violent crimes. In addition to providing immediate assistance, the police conduct investigations, secure crime scenes, and collaborate with emergency medical services when needed.

- **Investigation and Crime Solving:** Detectives within the PRPD focus on investigating crimes, collecting evidence, and identifying suspects. Specialized units address specific crimes such as cybercrime, counterterrorism, and human trafficking. They work closely with federal agencies like the FBI and DEA on cases involving federal jurisdiction.

- **Community Policing:** Both the PRPD and municipal police forces engage in community policing, building relationships with local residents and addressing quality-of-life issues. This helps foster trust between law enforcement and the community, which can improve cooperation in preventing and solving crimes.

Puerto Rico's police force faces several **significant challenges** that hinder its ability to respond effectively to crime and maintain public safety. One of the most pressing issues is **understaffing**, with the Puerto Rico Police Department (PRPD) stretched thin due to a high workload and limited resources. Officers often face long shifts, high caseloads, and budget cuts that affect equipment, training, and technology, making it harder to respond efficiently. The island also struggles with **high crime rates**, particularly drug trafficking, gang violence, and domestic violence, which place a heavy burden on law enforcement. Additionally, **corruption** and a lack of **accountability** within the police force have eroded public trust, with concerns about misconduct and ties to criminal organizations. This mistrust is compounded by a strained relationship between the police and the community, where incidents of **excessive use of force** have made cooperation more difficult. Officers also face increased **risks** due to violent encounters, further complicating recruitment and retention efforts. Together, these challenges undermine the police's ability to ensure safety and address crime effectively.

## Police and Community Relations

**The overall image and perception** of the police in Puerto Rico are **mixed**, shaped by a combination of historical, social, and institutional factors. While many residents acknowledge the police's efforts to combat crime and maintain public order, there are also significant concerns about corruption, misconduct, and the use of excessive force, which have contributed to a strained relationship between law enforcement and the community.

On one hand, the PRPD and local municipal police forces are seen as essential in tackling crime, especially given the island's struggles with high crime rates, including drug trafficking and gang violence. For many, police officers are viewed as critical to ensuring public safety, particularly in neighborhoods impacted by violence and criminal organizations. There are also positive perceptions of community policing efforts, where officers engage with residents and work to build trust, promote dialogue, and address local issues. However, the relationship is marred by incidents of **police misconduct, corruption**, and **abuse of power**.

There have been high-profile cases of police officers being involved in illegal activities or using excessive force, which have further damaged public trust. In some communities, particularly those in poorer areas, police presence is often associated with fear and suspicion rather than protection. Many Puerto Ricans feel that the police sometimes act more as enforcers than community partners, contributing to a perception of the force as distant or antagonistic.[46] Additionally, Puerto Rico's law enforcement has been under federal oversight due to concerns about corruption and accountability, which has further undermined public confidence. Efforts to reform the police force, such as introducing body cameras and focusing on improved training in de-escalation, aim to improve transparency and rebuild trust, but these initiatives have had mixed results.

Overall, while many people recognize the challenges faced by law enforcement in Puerto Rico, there is a **strong desire for reform**, better **accountability**, and a **more transparent relationship** between the police and the communities they serve. Public perception remains divided, and efforts to improve police-community relations will likely require a sustained commitment to addressing corruption, improving training, and fostering a more collaborative approach to law enforcement.

## Police Use of Force

The Puerto Rico Police Department has faced **long-standing accusations of excessive use of force**, particularly during protests and periods of civil unrest. Communities, especially those composed of **minority and low-income populations**, have frequently voiced concerns about being disproportionately targeted by law enforcement. Organizations like **Kilómetro Cero**, which focus on tracking police violence, have shown through rigorous data collection that incidents of lethal use-of-force are more frequent in predominantly nonwhite neighborhoods, regardless of income levels, and historical patterns indicate that especially individuals from poorer Afro-Caribbean neighborhoods are targeted most frequently.[47]

A report by the American Civil Liberties Union (ACLU) further documented a **culture of violence** and **impunity** within the PRPD. The

---

46  https://nacla.org/news/2019/05/23/policing-crisis#

47  https://www.urban.org/catalyst-grant-program-insights/shedding-light-police-violence-puerto-rico

investigation revealed systemic issues, including failures to hold officers accountable for misconduct, which eroded public trust in the force. Despite federal oversight and reforms implemented by the U.S. Department of Justice aimed at improving accountability and transparency, the PRPD has continued to grapple with these issues.

 **Law of the Land True Story**

On December 22, 2022, former Puerto Rico Police Officer Jose Cartagena, 47, was convicted of civil rights violations following a week-long trial. Cartagena was found guilty of assaulting a juvenile victim, identified as C.C., during an incident on November 15, 2014. Cartagena, along with other former officers, pursued C.C. on his bicycle. After the victim was apprehended and complied with police commands, Cartagena struck the handcuffed victim in the back of the head with a gun and continued to assault him while transporting him to the police station.

Cartagena was charged with two counts of depriving C.C. of his constitutional rights and two counts of obstruction of justice for falsifying a police report and making misleading statements to officials. The abuse led C.C. to seek medical treatment at a local hospital. Cartagena faces up to 20 years in prison and three other officers involved in the incident pleaded guilty to violating C.C.'s constitutional rights.

# HOW TO GET LEGAL HELP IN PUERTO RICO

# HOW TO GET LEGAL HELP IN PUERTO RICO

## Available Resources

If you are arrested in Puerto Rico, there are several important resources available to help you manage the situation and protect your rights. One of the first things to remember is your right to legal representation. If you cannot afford an attorney, a **public defender** will be appointed to you. The **Puerto Rico Bar Association** can also help you find a private attorney who can represent you if needed.

If you're a U.S. citizen, the **U.S. Consulate** in Puerto Rico can provide critical assistance. They can help you understand your legal rights, help you find local legal representation, and even assist with contacting your family members back home. In addition, the consulate can guide you through the legal process, ensuring that your treatment remains fair under Puerto Rican law. The U.S. Consulate in San Juan is the primary point of contact for any emergencies related to legal issues in Puerto Rico.

Regarding your detention, you have the right to request bail, depending on the charges. If bail is granted, you may contact a **bail bondsman** to arrange for your release. However, the decision to grant bail will depend on factors such as the nature of the charges and your risk of fleeing. Your constitutional rights are also protected, and if you experience mistreatment during your arrest or detention, you can file a formal complaint with the **Puerto Rico Civil Rights Commission** or the **Internal Affairs Division** of the Puerto Rico Police Department. Both entities are responsible for investigating abuses or violations of rights by law enforcement.

If you are struggling emotionally or mentally due to your situation, you can request access to mental health professionals. Puerto Rico has several mental health organizations and support groups that provide counseling for detainees who need help coping with their circumstances.

If language barriers are an issue, you are entitled to a **translator** who will ensure that you fully understand the legal process, the charges against you, and your rights. This service is important, especially if you are not fluent in Spanish.

In addition to government support, there are several **non-governmental organizations** (NGOs) in Puerto Rico that offer legal aid and other forms of assistance. **Puerto Rico Legal Services**, for example, provides free legal support to those who cannot afford an attorney, while the **American Civil Liberties Union** (ACLU) of Puerto Rico operates hotlines that provide legal information and advice regarding civil rights and police encounters. Such services can be invaluable for individuals seeking immediate help or clarity about their rights during an arrest.

By utilizing these resources, you can ensure that your rights are upheld and that you have access to the support you need during a difficult time. Whether it's through legal assistance, mental health services, or help from the U.S. Consulate, Puerto Rico offers several pathways to ensure that those who are arrested receive fair treatment under the law.

## Legal Aid

Foreign visitors to Puerto Rico may be eligible for legal aid, but this largely depends on their specific legal situation and immigration status. Generally, legal aid is available to low-income individuals who demonstrate a need for assistance.[48] Foreign visitors must prove their financial

---

48  https://gottrouble.org/puerto-rico-legal-aid-and-pro-bono-services/

need, often with income-based documentation or proof of hardship. However, **legal aid services are primarily intended for residents and legal immigrants, and visitors, especially tourists without ties to the community, may face limitations based on their immigration status.**

To apply for legal aid, foreign visitors must first contact a legal aid organization or the local Office of the Public Defender and provide documentation related to their legal issue, financial status, and identification. The process typically includes completing an **intake form**, where applicants disclose personal and economic information. **Eligibility screening** follows, considering income and, in the case of foreign visitors, immigration status. If qualified, applicants are **matched with an attorney** who can provide legal assistance.

**Eligibility criteria** generally include income below a set threshold, often based on federal poverty guidelines, and the nature of the legal issue, which typically involves civil matters like housing, family law, or immigration issues. Criminal cases may also be eligible for public defender services. Applicants are often required to show some form of residency or legal presence in Puerto Rico, which may be a challenge for foreign visitors.[49]

Legal aid services in Puerto Rico offer a variety of support, including **legal representation** in civil cases, **consultations** about rights and legal processes, **case management**, and **educational workshops**.[50] These services aim to help individuals navigate the legal system, ensuring they receive necessary assistance even in complex legal matters.

## Foreign Embassies in Puerto Rico

Embassies and consulates in Puerto Rico serve as **vital points of contact for citizens from foreign countries**, helping them with consular services such as issuing passports, providing visa assistance, supporting citizens during emergencies (e.g., medical, legal, or travel issues), and

---

49 https://www.statedepartment.pr.gov/foreigners

50 https://www.ladrc.org/state-and-territory-resources/puerto-rico/

offering help in cases of arrest or detention. In addition to these services, embassies and consulates also play a key role in fostering diplomatic relations, promoting trade and cultural exchanges, and informing the public about their home country's laws, policies, and services. While embassies handle broader diplomatic and political matters, consulates focus on more localized and practical assistance for citizens within specific regions.

Puerto Rico, as a U.S. territory, does not host as many foreign embassies as independent countries, but it does have several consular offices representing different nations. The U.S. Embassy itself is located in Washington, D.C., but consulates are present in Puerto Rico to serve the local foreign communities. Puerto Rico's consular offices provide a wide range of services for nationals residing on the island, as well as for visitors in need of assistance.

The **consular presence** in Puerto Rico is **mostly concentrated in San Juan**, the capital and largest city, but some countries also have consulates or honorary consulates in other locations. Here are the contact details for some of the key consulates operating in Puerto Rico:

### Consulate of the Dominican Republic

Phone: (787) 756-8000

Email: consuladodominicano@gmail.com

### Consulate of Colombia

Phone: (787) 294-6717

Email: csanjuan@cancilleria.gov.co

### Consulate of Canada

Phone: (787) 759-6629

Email: canadapr@worldnet.att.net

### Consulate of Mexico

Phone: (787) 764-0258

Email: cgmexico-sanjuan@sre.gob.mx

## Consulate of Spain

Phone: (787) 758-6279
Email: cgesp.pr@correo.mae.es

 For a more detailed list of all the consulates in Puerto Rico, please visit **https://welcome.topuertorico.org/reference/consulates.shtml**.

# MEDICAL FACILITIES & HOSPITALS

CHAPTER 17
# MEDICAL FACILITIES & HOSPITALS

## Overview

Healthcare in Puerto Rico operates within a **dual system** of public and private services. This system is largely shaped by the U.S. federal programs, but it is modified by the unique economic and political context of the island.

The *Mi Salud* program is the backbone of Puerto Rico's **public healthcare system**. This program, similar to Medicaid on the U.S. mainland, provides comprehensive healthcare services to a significant portion of the population, particularly those with low incomes, the elderly, and people with disabilities. Mi Salud covers **essential services such as primary care, emergency care, hospital services, preventive services like vaccinations, and prescription medications**. However, the program is **underfunded** compared to Medicaid in the states, and its reimbursement rates to healthcare providers are lower. As a result, many doctors and healthcare facilities are hesitant to accept Mi Salud patients, contributing to limited access to care for those who rely on the program.

Puerto Rico also participates in the **Medicare** program, which provides health coverage for individuals aged 65 and older. While Medicare beneficiaries in Puerto Rico receive the same basic coverage as those on the mainland, the reimbursement rates for Medicare on the island are lower, creating challenges for providers and potentially leading to gaps in service quality.

In addition to Mi Salud and Medicare, **Federally Qualified Health Centers (FQHCs)** play a critical role in the public healthcare system. These centers are located throughout the island, often in underserved or rural areas, and provide essential primary care services, dental care, mental health services, and substance abuse treatment. FQHCs are particularly important for uninsured individuals or those who cannot afford to seek care at private hospitals or clinics.

**Private healthcare** in Puerto Rico is well-developed, particularly in urban centers like San Juan. Wealthier individuals or those with employer-sponsored insurance typically have access to private healthcare services, which are perceived to offer higher-quality care. Private hospitals, such as **Pavia Hospitals** and **San Juan City Hospital**, provide a wide range of specialized medical services and are equipped with the latest technologies. These hospitals tend to have shorter wait times, more personalized care, and greater availability of specialized medical professionals.

However, private healthcare is **not accessible to everyone**. While it serves a significant portion of the population, it is often out of reach for lower-income residents, who may not have private insurance or the financial means to pay out-of-pocket for services. For many Puerto Ricans, the choice between public and private healthcare is dictated by financial circumstances, with many families relying on Mi Salud or government subsidies to cover healthcare costs.

Puerto Rico's healthcare system shares **many similarities with the U.S. mainland**, offering high-quality care in major cities like San Juan, where private hospitals provide advanced treatments and state-of-the-art technologies. Notable hospitals such as Hospital de la Concepción and Hospital Auxilio Mutuo are known for their specialized care. However, these **high standards** are **not evenly distributed across the island**. Economic challenges, including a long-standing debt crisis, have strained government resources, leading to underfunding of public health programs and the deterioration of public hospitals, which suffer from outdated equipment and long wait times.

Additionally, Puerto Rico faces a **significant shortage of healthcare professionals**, with many leaving for better opportunities on the mainland.

This has created workforce gaps, particularly in rural areas, where residents often experience reduced access to specialized care and longer wait times. While Puerto Rico has made progress in improving public health, with gains in life expectancy, reductions in childhood mortality, and advancements in the fight against infectious diseases, chronic conditions such as diabetes, hypertension, and heart disease remain prevalent, and health outcomes continue to vary significantly based on socio-economic and geographic factors, highlighting ongoing health disparities.

## Visitors' Access to Healthcare in Puerto Rico

When visiting Puerto Rico, understanding how to access healthcare services is essential in case of an emergency or medical need. While Puerto Rico is a U.S. territory, and its healthcare system mirrors many aspects of mainland U.S. practices, there are important details and differences to consider.

If you're a U.S. citizen visiting Puerto Rico, your **U.S. health insurance plan should generally provide coverage for medical services on the island.** Since Puerto Rico is part of the United States, most U.S. health insurance plans cover **emergency care, hospital visits**, and other **necessary medical services.** However, there may be some restrictions depending on the type of insurance. Some insurance plans have **in-network** and **out-of-network** providers, so it's important to **confirm with your insurance provider** which doctors and hospitals are covered in Puerto Rico. Also, your insurance might cover emergency care but not routine medical visits, so it's essential to check whether your plan covers the type of care you might need.

**Medicare** beneficiaries can use their coverage in Puerto Rico, as Puerto Ricans are covered by Medicare just like U.S. residents. However, the **funding for Medicare in Puerto Rico** is lower than in the mainland U.S., which may affect the availability or quality of care in certain facilities.

The **Medicaid program in Puerto Rico** (known as *Mi Salud*) is **primarily for Puerto Rican residents.** Visitors, tourists, or short-term travelers would not be eligible for coverage under Mi Salud. **Visitors will need other forms of insurance or will have to pay out-of-pocket.**

Foreign insurance plans are generally accepted in Puerto Rico, particularly at private hospitals. Since Puerto Rico is a U.S. territory, many healthcare facilities accept **international health insurance** and **U.S. plans.** However, it's important to verify coverage with your insurer before traveling to ensure you are covered for medical services in Puerto Rico, especially for emergencies or specialized care.

**Public healthcare** services, provided by government-run hospitals and clinics, may be **more affordable** than private care. However, public hospitals often face **longer wait times** and may not offer the same level of specialized care. Visitors should also be aware that **public health services are generally designed for Puerto Rican residents, so there may be differences in service quality or access for tourists.**

**In an emergency,** you will typically need to **pay for services at the point of care.** This includes ambulance rides, which are often not covered by all insurance policies. If you don't have health insurance that covers emergency transport, you'll need to pay for the ambulance ride **out-of-pocket.** Emergency rooms (ER) in both private and public hospitals will treat you, but you'll need to pay for the services rendered either through insurance or directly.

Visitors can access **emergency rooms** in Puerto Rico just as they would on the mainland. **Emergency care is available at both private and public hospitals, and ERs are generally open 24/7.** However, visitors should be aware that **insurance coverage may vary,** particularly at private facilities. Out-of-pocket payments for ER visits can be expensive if your insurance does not cover the hospital or your medical needs.

Visitors can fill **prescriptions** in Puerto Rico just like they would in the mainland U.S. Many major pharmacy chains, such as **CVS, Walgreens,** and **Rite Aid,** have locations on the island, and most **local pharmacies will accept U.S. prescriptions.** However, if you are uninsured or your plan does not cover prescription drugs in Puerto Rico, you will need to pay **out-of-pocket**. Prices for prescriptions may vary depending on the medication.

*Key Considerations for Visitors*

- **Language:** Spanish is the primary language in Puerto Rico, but most healthcare providers in larger cities speak English, which can be helpful for visitors. For international visitors, medical facilities catering to tourism typically offer language assistance to ensure smooth communication and access to care.

- **Quality of Care:** Private hospitals generally offer **high-quality care**, but public hospitals may have **longer wait times** and limited access to specialized services.

- **Healthcare Access:** While **San Juan** and other urban areas have a wide range of medical facilities, visitors in more remote areas may face limited access to healthcare services and may need to travel to larger cities for advanced care.

## Puerto Rico's Hospitals

As of recent reports, Puerto Rico is home to approximately **64 general hospitals** that serve both urban and rural populations across the island.[51] These hospitals range from large, fully equipped facilities to smaller community hospitals, providing varied levels of care and specialty services. Additionally, the healthcare system includes specialized medical centers, long-term care facilities, and urgent care centers, further contributing to the island's healthcare capacity.

In terms of **medical staffing**, the healthcare workforce in Puerto Rico has faced significant challenges over the past decades, particularly due to physician migration to the United States mainland. The number of **practicing physicians** in Puerto Rico has **dramatically declined** from about 14,500 in 2009 to around 9,000 in 2020, indicating a substantial decrease of about 38 percent in just over a decade, a trend that continues

---

51   https://pmc.ncbi.nlm.nih.gov/articles/PMC11294551/

today.[52] This trend not only affects the quality and availability of health-care services but also creates a strain on the remaining medical staff, as the demand for services continues to rise. According to estimates, there are approximately 20,000 to 25,000 nurses working in Puerto Rico, with a significant concentration in urban centers. Nurse-to-patient ratios in rural areas can sometimes be challenging as the rural hospitals tend to be severely understaffed.

*Most Prominent Hospitals*

Puerto Rico's healthcare system offers a variety of public and private hospitals that cater to both local residents and international visitors. Among the top private hospitals are **Auxilio Mutuo Hospital**, known for its advanced medical technology and medical tourism certification; **Ashford Presbyterian Community Hospital**, celebrated for its trauma and emergency care; **HIMA San Pablo Hospital**, which specializes in cardiology and orthopedics; and **Doctors' Center Hospital**, recognized for its high patient satisfaction and advanced diagnostics. On the public side, **Centro Médico de Puerto Rico**, the island's largest healthcare facility, provides comprehensive tertiary care, and **Hospital Universitario Dr. Ramón Ruiz Arnau** in Bayamón offers a range of specialty services. Hospitals like **Auxilio Mutuo** and **Ashford Presbyterian** cater specifically to international visitors by providing services such as language assistance, medical tourism logistics, and English-speaking staff. These hospitals offer comprehensive care packages designed to make the medical experience more seamless for international patients.

 **Medical Emergencies**

1. **What should you do if you feel unwell/sick in Puerto Rico?** If you feel unwell in Puerto Rico, assess your symptoms and, for minor issues, visit a pharmacy for over-the-counter remedies. For

---

52  https://pmc.ncbi.nlm.nih.gov/articles/PMC11294551

more serious conditions, seek care at a private hospital or clinic, especially in San Juan, where English-speaking staff is common. In an emergency, call **911** for immediate assistance, with hospitals like Auxilio Mutuo providing 24/7 care. If you have travel insurance, contact your provider for coverage details. Many hospitals also offer specialized services and support for international visitors.

2. **Are there any specialized medical facilities in Puerto Rico for travelers who need urgent care or evacuation services?**
**Yes.** In Puerto Rico, several medical facilities handle urgent care and evacuations for travelers. **Hospital Pavia** in Santurce, **Centro Médico de Puerto Rico**, and **Auxilio Mutuo** Hospital in San Juan offer comprehensive emergency services and can arrange medical evacuations if needed. **San Juan Medical Center** also provides urgent care with a focus on international patients. For critical cases requiring air or ground evacuation, specialized air ambulance services are available. Travelers should ensure their insurance covers medical emergencies and evacuations.

 Here are the most important emergency numbers you should place in your phone while in Puerto Rico:[53]

- **Emergency Services:** 911
- **Police (non-emergency):** 787-343-2020
- **Ambulance:** 787-343-2222
- **Civil Defense:** 787-724-0124
- **Fire Department:** 787-343-2330
- **U.S. Coast Guard:** 787-729-6770

53  https://welcome.topuertorico.org/emergency.shtml

## Insurance Guidance[54]

For visitors coming from outside the U.S. or those without insurance that covers Puerto Rico, purchasing **travel health insurance** is a good option. This insurance typically covers **emergency medical expenses, hospitalization**, and sometimes **medical evacuation** if you become seriously ill or injured. Travel insurance ensures you are covered for unexpected medical events, especially when your regular health insurance doesn't extend to Puerto Rico.

If visitors do not have insurance or their insurance doesn't fully cover Puerto Rico, they can pay **out-of-pocket** for healthcare services. Private hospitals and clinics in Puerto Rico will usually require proof of insurance or payment upfront. The cost of medical services in private facilities is similar to what one might expect in the U.S., though prices can vary depending on the care required (e.g., consultations, diagnostics, hospital stays). Payment options generally include **cash, credit/debit cards**, or **insurance**. For non-emergency care, it's important to **inquire about the costs upfront**, as medical bills can accumulate quickly if you're not prepared. Most hospitals and clinics will provide an **estimate of costs** before treatment.

The costs for medical services in Puerto Rico can vary depending on the type of care and the facility. On average:

- **Emergency Room Visit:** Around **US$300 to $1,000** for a basic visit, with additional costs for tests or treatments.

- **Doctor's Visit:** Typically ranges from **US$50 to $150** for a consultation with a general practitioner.

- **Specialist Consultation:** Can range from **US$100 to $300** depending on the specialty.

- **Hospital Stay:** The daily cost for a hospital stay is generally between **US$1,000 to $3,000** per day, depending on the severity of care needed.

---

54  https://www.internations.org/costa-rica-expats/guide/healthcare

If your foreign insurance covers Puerto Rico, you may need to provide your insurance details upfront. Some hospitals accept direct billing, while others may require you to pay first and seek reimbursement. For those without insurance, services are usually paid for directly via **cash**, **credit card**, or **debit card**. Some facilities may offer **payment plans** or financial assistance options, especially for larger bills. However, it's always a good idea to inquire about costs before treatment to avoid unexpected bills.

# DRIVING IN PUERTO RICO

# DRIVING IN PUERTO RICO

## Overview[55]

Driving in Puerto Rico offers a unique experience, shaped by a combination of modern infrastructure in urban areas and more challenging roads in rural regions. In cities like San Juan, the driving experience can be hectic, especially during rush hours, when traffic congestion is common. The roadways in urban centers are generally in good condition, with well-maintained traffic signs and signals. However, finding parking can be a challenge, particularly in crowded areas, where visitors often have to rely on parking garages or paid street parking. Outside of the city, the roads become quieter but may be more difficult to navigate. In more remote or mountainous regions, roads can be narrow, winding, and sometimes poorly lit at night, requiring extra caution.

Puerto Rico's road infrastructure is overall quite solid, especially along major highways and interstates like PR-22 and PR-52, which are well-paved and connect the main cities and tourist hotspots. While most of the primary roads are in good shape, some rural areas may have roads that are less well-maintained, with occasional potholes or uneven surfaces. Highways, such as PR-52, may include tolls, but they provide efficient routes across the island. The signage on roads is typically clear, with both English and Spanish instructions, though it can be less visible in more remote areas.

---

55  https://www.conquistadortravels.com/post/driving-in-puerto-rico-101

Puerto Rico's tropical climate can also play a role in driving conditions, particularly during the rainy season. Heavy rains can cause flooding, especially in lower-lying areas, and make certain mountain roads slippery or difficult to drive. Visitors should exercise extra caution during storms or after heavy rainfall. While Puerto Rico follows similar traffic laws to the mainland U.S., including seatbelt use and DUI regulations, local driving habits can sometimes be aggressive, and speed limits may be exceeded on less congested roads.

Road safety in Puerto Rico is generally in line with U.S. standards, but visitors should remain aware of a few local nuances. Speed limits are posted clearly, and seat belt use is mandatory for all passengers. Driving under the influence is strictly prohibited, with severe penalties for violations. While traffic signs and signals are mostly effective, enforcement can vary, and visitors should be especially cautious in urban areas where pedestrian traffic is common. Rural roads may have potholes or uneven surfaces, particularly after heavy rain, and some mountainous routes can be narrow and winding, requiring extra attention. Flooding is a concern after rainstorms, and it's important to avoid driving during heavy rainfall. In rural areas, wildlife and stray animals can pose hazards. Visitors should use headlights in low-visibility conditions, carry an emergency kit, and always follow parking regulations to avoid fines. Overall, Puerto Rico's road safety requires vigilance, especially in more remote areas, but with proper precautions, visitors can navigate the island safely.

## Document and Insurance Requirements for Foreign Drivers

Foreign visitors planning to drive in Puerto Rico must meet certain requirements. First, a valid driver's license from their home country is generally accepted, but it is advisable to also carry an International Driving Permit (IDP), especially if the license is not in English or Spanish. The IDP translates the information on the driver's license into multiple languages, which may be helpful if you need to interact with local authorities.

For visitors from the U.S. mainland, a standard U.S. driver's license is sufficient to drive in Puerto Rico, as it follows the same driving laws and regulations. However, non-U.S. residents or foreign nationals should verify with their rental car agency if they need an IDP in addition to their foreign license, though many companies will accept a foreign license alone.

Regarding car insurance, U.S. visitors' insurance coverage is generally valid in Puerto Rico. However, foreign visitors should check with their home insurance provider to ensure their policy covers Puerto Rico. Rental car agencies will typically offer insurance options, including a Collision Damage Waiver (CDW), theft protection, and third-party liability insurance. It's highly recommended to purchase insurance through the rental agency to avoid any complications, as your own foreign insurance might not be recognized by local authorities or rental companies. If you plan to use a credit card for car rentals, check whether the card offers rental insurance coverage for driving in Puerto Rico.

*Toll Roads in Puerto Rico*

Puerto Rico has **several toll roads**, primarily concentrated along major highways like **PR-22**, **PR-52**, and **PR-66**, which help connect cities and regions efficiently. Tolls are commonly used to fund maintenance and upgrades to the infrastructure. Toll booths are automated, and visitors will encounter both manual and electronic toll collection systems.

**Tolls** can be paid in **cash**, typically in U.S. dollars. Exact change is often required, though some toll booths may give change for larger bills. It's a good idea to carry small bills or coins to speed up the payment process. Puerto Rico uses an **electronic toll collection** system known as "**AutoExpreso.**" This system involves a small transponder placed in the vehicle, which automatically deducts the toll fee as you drive through the toll booth. Visitors can rent an AutoExpreso tag from the rental car company or purchase one at authorized kiosks on the island. The tag will be linked to the car rental agreement, and tolls will be charged to the driver's credit card or rental account. Some toll booths also accept credit cards, particularly in more developed areas, but cash and AutoExpreso are the most commonly used methods.

 ## Main Traffic Rules

- **Driving side:** Vehicles drive on the right side of the road.

- **Speed limits:** Residential areas - 25 mph, Urban areas - 30-40 mph, Highways - 65 mph.

- **Seat belts:** Mandatory for all passengers.

- **Alcohol:** BAC limit is 0.08 percent; driving under the influence is illegal.

- **Mobile devices:** Prohibited unless hands-free.

- **Toll roads:** Cash and AutoExpreso transponder accepted.

- **Road safety tips:** Watch for pedestrians, use headlights in low-visibility, and avoid flooded roads.

- **Road safety:** Be cautious of potholes, narrow mountain roads, and stray animals.

## General Questions

1. *Can I use my driver's license from my home country to drive in Puerto Rico?* **Yes.** You can use your driver's license from your home country to drive in Puerto Rico. However, it is recommended to carry an **International Driving Permit** (**IDP**) if your license is not in English or Spanish. For U.S. citizens, a standard U.S. driver's license is sufficient. Make sure to check with your rental car agency to confirm if an IDP is required.

2. *What is the age requirement for renting a car in Puerto Rico?* The minimum age to rent a car in Puerto Rico is typically **21 years old**. However, drivers under 25 may be subject to a **young driver surcharge**. Some rental agencies may have a minimum age of 25, and restrictions may apply to those under 21, particularly for luxury or specialty vehicles. Be sure to check with the rental agency for specific requirements.

## Law of the Land Hypothetical

HYPOTHETICAL: *Maria, a 22-year-old tourist from New York, is planning a vacation to Puerto Rico. She's excited to explore the island and decides to rent a car for her trip. Maria calls a local rental agency and when she mentions her age, the agent informs her that the minimum age to rent a car is 21, but drivers under 25 may be subject to an additional **young driver surcharge**. Maria asks if she can rent a luxury vehicle, and the agent advises her that rental agencies typically restrict drivers under 25 from renting specialty cars like convertibles or sports cars. Maria wonders if these restrictions are standard across all rental agencies in Puerto Rico or if she might be able to find one that allows her to rent a luxury car.*

ANSWER: *Maria may not be able to rent a luxury or specialty vehicle, such as a sports car or convertible, from most rental agencies in Puerto*

*Rico due to her age. While the minimum age for renting a standard ve-hicle is typically 21, rental agencies often impose additional age-relat-ed restrictions on luxury or specialty cars for drivers under 25. These restrictions vary by agency, so Maria should check with the specific rental agency to see if they offer an exception or alternative options. It's also important for Maria to inquire about any **young driver sur-charges**, as those may apply to her rental.*

CHAPTER 19
# NUDE BEACHES &
# CLOTHING-OPTIONAL RESORTS

CHAPTER 19

# NUDE BEACHES & CLOTHING-OPTIONAL RESORTS

## Overview

In Puerto Rico, **nudism isn't widely accepted** in mainstream culture, which tends to be more **conservative** due to the island's **strong Catholic influences** and **traditional values.** Public nudity isn't something you'll see often, and while the island is known for its relaxed vibe, it's still generally expected that you wear clothing in public spaces.

However, there are a **few remote beaches** where **nudism is more tolerated**, though it's important to remember that these are not officially designated as "clothing-optional" beaches. They are just quieter, more secluded spots where naturists may choose to strip down without drawing too much attention.

One such place is **Playa Escondida** near Rincón. This beach is somewhat hidden, making it a popular spot for those looking for solitude and a more relaxed atmosphere. The area is remote enough that some people choose to be nude, though it's not officially sanctioned. Another spot that attracts nudists is **Playa Flamenco** on Culebra, a well-known beach with stunning scenery. While it's not an official nude beach, the further you walk from the main area, the more you might find people practicing naturism, particularly in the more secluded sections. Similarly, **Playa de la Esperanza** on Vieques is a quiet, less-visited beach where some people choose to go nude. Like the others, it's not officially a nude beach, but it's a place where nudity is less likely to cause a stir.

That said, even at these quieter spots, it's important to be respectful of local norms. **Puerto Rico doesn't have any designated clothing-optional beaches, so nudism is generally only tolerated in more isolated areas.** In popular or crowded beaches, it would be considered inappropriate.

If you're looking for a more openly accepting nudist culture, Puerto Rico might not be the place. However, if you prefer to embrace nature in a more private, secluded environment, there are spots where you can enjoy the freedom of nudism without much interference. Just be aware of your surroundings and respectful of others.

## Legality and Safety

Puerto Rican law explicitly **prohibits public nudity**, categorizing it as an **offense against public decency.** According to the "indecent exposure" statute codified in Puerto Rican law, an individual may incur a misdemeanor for exposing intimate parts of the body in a public setting where it can potentially offend or upset others, including law enforcement personnel.[56] This legal definition highlights the rigidity of public nudity regulations in Puerto Rico, demonstrating a clear limitation in the practice of nudism on public beaches or spaces where others might be present.

While the island's relaxed atmosphere and stunning beaches might seem like an ideal setting for naturism, public nudity is not openly accepted in most places. If someone chooses to be nude in public, they could face legal consequences, including fines or even arrest, especially if their actions are considered a disturbance or offense to others.[57] That being said, in more remote, secluded areas—such as certain parts of **Playa Escondida** near Rincón or **Playa Flamenco** on Culebra—nudism may be tolerated

---

56  https://casetext.com/statute/laws-of-puerto-rico/title-thirty-three-penal-code/subtitle-5-penal-code-of-2004-special-provisions/part-i-crimes-against-the-person/chapter-300

57  https://www.beachatlas.com/nudism-laws-puerto-rico

to some extent. These places are far from crowded, and local authorities are less likely to enforce indecent exposure laws as strictly. However, this tolerance is more about isolation and a lack of enforcement rather than any formal legal protection for nudists. In busier, tourist-heavy spots, such as in San Juan or popular public beaches, nudity is less likely to be accepted, and authorities will more actively intervene if someone is found to be nude in public spaces.

If you're on private property, such as in a vacation rental or a secluded area on the beach, nudism is generally allowed, provided it doesn't encroach on public spaces. But the moment your nudity becomes visible to others or causes a disruption, you could run into legal issues.

Ultimately, given these legal restrictions and cultural expectations, those who choose to engage in nudism in Puerto Rico **must exercise discretion** and **respect for local customs**. Practicing nudism in public spaces, even in remote areas, is a grey zone and should be done with caution. Being mindful of other beachgoers, staying in less conspicuous parts of secluded beaches, and avoiding attracting attention can help minimize the risk of confrontation with authorities or the local community. The lack of official protections and the conservative nature of Puerto Rican society means that naturists must be prepared for potential challenges when embracing this lifestyle on the island.

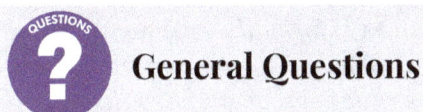 **General Questions**

1. *Are there any local groups or organizations in Puerto Rico that advocate for nudism or naturism, and do they offer guidance on safe and respectful places to visit?* Puerto Rico does not have a large, formally organized naturist or nudist community like those found in other countries. However, there are **smaller, informal groups** and **online communities** where people who practice nudism share tips and recommendations. Websites, social media pages, and online forums such as Facebook groups or Reddit threads related to Puerto Rican travel or naturism

often provide guidance on specific beaches that are more tolerant of nudism, like Playa Escondida or Playa Flamenco. While these spaces may not have official backing, the discussions in these online communities can help you find secluded and respectful locations. Still, **it's important to keep in mind that these areas are not legally protected, and any information should be taken with caution.**

2. ***What are some common misconceptions about nudism in Puerto Rico that people might have before visiting?*** A common misconception is that nudism is widely accepted or practiced in Puerto Rico due to its laid-back beach culture. While some secluded beaches may tolerate nudity, it is **not widespread or publicly accepted.** There are no official clothing-optional beaches or resorts, and public nudity can lead to legal consequences or social discomfort. Despite the island's relaxed vibe, Puerto Rican culture still holds strong traditional values around modesty and decency.

 **Law of the Land Hypothetical**

HYPOTHETICAL: *Sophia and her friends visit Playa Flamenco on Culebra, having heard that nudism is informally tolerated in some parts of the beach. They set up in a secluded area and start sunbathing nude. However, a family with young children soon arrives nearby, and the parents begin giving them uncomfortable looks. Sophia starts feeling self-conscious and wonders whether they should cover up or move. What should Sophia do to be respectful of local customs and others while practicing nudism in Puerto Rico?*

ANSWER: *Sophia should be mindful of the family's presence and respect their comfort level. Although nudism may be tolerated in certain areas of Playa Flamenco, it's important to consider the cultural context, as Puerto Rican society tends to be more conservative. In this case, Sophia should either cover up or move to a more secluded area to avoid making others uncomfortable. By doing so, she can help maintain a positive environment and avoid any awkward situations while still enjoying the beach.*

LAW OF THE LAND PUERTO RICO

# UNUSUAL LAWS

- Overview
- Puerto Rico's Unusual Laws and Associated Penalties
- General Questions
- Law of the Land Hypothetical

# UNUSUAL LAWS

## Overview

Unusual laws can be fascinating glimpses into a culture's values and history. While most people are aware of common legal restrictions, it's often the strange and quirky laws that capture our attention. These regulations can range from the amusing to the absurd, reflecting the unique circumstances and traditions of a place. Whether they arise from historical events, societal norms, or simply peculiar local customs, unusual laws can provide insight into the quirks of human behavior and governance.

## Puerto Rico's Unusual Laws and Associated Penalties

Puerto Rico, as a U.S. territory, blends a unique mix of American legal principles with local customs and traditions. While many of its laws align with those in the U.S., there are a few that stand out as unusual or quirky, often reflecting the island's rich cultural history and specific regional needs. Whether it's a law that speaks to public decency or one tied to local customs, these unique regulations can catch visitors off guard if they're not familiar with them. From restrictions on public nudity to curfews for minors, here are a few examples of Puerto

Rico's more unexpected laws and the penalties that come with breaking them:

- **Curfew for Minors:** There is a curfew law in place for minors (under 18 years old) in Puerto Rico. Typically, the curfew is from **10:00 PM to 5:00 AM**, with exceptions for certain activities like work, travel with a guardian, or emergencies. If a minor is found violating the curfew, they may be detained by law enforcement, and their parents or guardians could be fined. The penalty for minors can include a **warning**, and for parents, a **fine** can be imposed, which varies depending on the situation.

- **Illegal to Sing Christmas Carols After Epiphany (January 6):** This quirky law stems from traditional Puerto Rican culture, which emphasizes that Christmas celebrations should end by **January 6th** (the Day of the Epiphany). Singing Christmas carols beyond this date is technically against the law. Though rarely enforced, breaking this law could technically result in a **fine** or **penalty**, though in practice, this is more of a cultural guideline than a law that is strictly enforced.

- **The Gag Law (Ley de la Mordaza):** Enacted in 1948, the Gag Law, or Ley de la Mordaza, made it illegal to display or own a Puerto Rican flag, even in private. This law was designed to suppress the island's independence movement and allowed authorities to search homes without a warrant if they suspected violations. Violators could face **imprisonment** or **hefty fines**. The law instilled fear and repression until it was repealed in 1957, though its impact on Puerto Rican memory and freedom is still felt today.[58]

- **Discrimination Based on Hairstyles:** Puerto Rico passed the Law Against Discrimination Based on Hairstyles in 2024, prohibiting discrimination in employment, education, housing, and public services based on protective hairstyles such as locs, cornrows, and afros. Employers violating this law may face **fines**

---

58  https://www.wlvt.org/blogs/lehigh/
    ley-de-la-mordaza-the-law-that-made-the-puerto-rican-flag-illegal/

of up to **US$10,000** for repeated offenses. Individuals facing discrimination can seek civil actions and redress in court.[59]

- **No Serving Food Without a Toilet:** In Puerto Rico, it's illegal for food service establishments like restaurants, bars, or cafés to operate without a functioning restroom for patrons. Violating this law can lead to the **temporary closure** of the establishment and **fines** imposed by health inspectors until the issue is resolved.

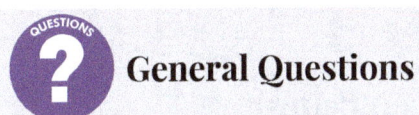 ## General Questions

1. *How do unusual laws, like the "no serving food without a toilet" rule, shape daily life and business operations in Puerto Rico?* These quirky laws, like the one requiring restaurants to have a functioning restroom, ensure that businesses maintain hygiene and safety standards. They might seem odd, but they help keep public spaces clean and protect public health. For business owners, it means adding extra costs and effort to comply with regulations, but it also ensures customers have a better overall experience.

2. *How has Puerto Rico's legal history, like the Gag Law, influenced the way locals view freedom of expression today?* The Gag Law, which suppressed the display of the Puerto Rican flag and cracked down on pro-independence movements, left a lasting impact on Puerto Rican identity. Today, people in Puerto Rico are more vocal about their pride in their culture and history. The law's repeal in 1957 marked a turning point, and it has shaped the island's strong sense of independence and desire for self-expression, especially in political and cultural matters.

---

59  https://www.jacksonlewis.com/insights/
puerto-rico-enacts-law-against-discrimination-based-hairstyles

3. *What kind of difference has the new law against discrimination based on hairstyles made for people in Puerto Rico?* The new law, which protects against discrimination based on protective hairstyles like afros, cornrows, and locs, has made a big difference for many people in Puerto Rico, especially in schools and workplaces. It helps ensure that individuals can express their cultural identity without facing bias or prejudice. For many, it's seen as **a step toward greater inclusivity and respect for diversity**, giving people more confidence in how they present themselves without worrying about discrimination.

 ## Law of the Land Hypothetical

**HYPOTHETICAL**: *Alex opens a café in San Juan, but he faces two issues. First, a health inspector informs him that his café could be shut down because it lacks a functioning restroom, which is required by law for all food establishments. Second, a customer complains about one of Alex's staff members, Maria, wearing an afro, claiming it makes them uncomfortable.*

*Can Alex be fined or forced to close his café for not having a restroom, and is he legally obligated to address the complaint about Maria's afro hairstyle?*

**ANSWER**: *Yes. Alex can face a **temporary closure** and **fines** if he doesn't fix the restroom issue as required by law. However, he cannot be penalized for allowing Maria to wear her afro, as Puerto Rico's law against discrimination based on hairstyles protects employees from bias related to their natural or protective hairstyles. The customer's discomfort doesn't provide legal grounds to take action against Maria.*

CHAPTER 21

# TRAVELING SAFELY

# TRAVELING SAFELY

## Ladies Traveling Solo[60]

Puerto Rico is a popular travel destination for solo travelers, offering a mix of vibrant culture, stunning beaches, and rich history. The island's reputation, in general, leans toward being a **relatively safe destination for tourists**, but like any other place, it's important to be aware of **local safety nuances**, especially for women traveling alone. Puerto Rico's tourism industry is strong, and the majority of travelers, including solo women, report positive experiences. However, as with any popular tourist destination, there are areas and situations that require more caution.

For the most part, Puerto Rico's major tourist areas like **Old San Juan, Condado, Isla Verde**, and **Rincón** are considered **safe for women traveling alone.** These areas are bustling with tourists, locals, and plenty of amenities, so they feel lively and well-patrolled. In these spots, solo travelers can often blend in without drawing attention and enjoy all the natural beauty and culture the island has to offer.

That said, there are **certain precautions** women should take to stay safe. There are neighborhoods, especially in San Juan, that are known for higher crime rates, such as parts of **Santurce** or **Bayamón**. These areas tend to be less touristy and may not be ideal for solo travelers, particularly after dark. It's also wise to stay away from **remote areas** that

---

60  https://www.worldpackers.com/articles/is-puerto-rico-safe

are not frequently traveled by locals or tourists, especially after the sun sets. Some secluded beaches or hiking trails, while beautiful, may not be well-policed or safe at night.

In terms of general safety for women, Puerto Rico is much like any other tourist destination—**being cautious and aware of your surroundings is key**. Women traveling solo are often advised to avoid walking alone at night in poorly lit or less populated areas. Taxis or ridesharing services like Uber are good alternatives to walking long distances, especially after dark.

Another tip for solo travelers is to avoid displaying expensive items such as jewelry or cameras, as this can attract unwanted attention. While Puerto Rico is generally safe, petty thefts like pickpocketing can happen in crowded places or on public transportation, especially in busy areas like **Plaza Las Américas** or near popular beaches.

Puerto Rico is also known for its warm hospitality, and locals are often willing to help if you need directions or advice. It's not uncommon for solo travelers to strike up conversations with friendly locals, especially in tourist-heavy spots. Nevertheless, it's always best to trust your instincts. If a situation or person feels uncomfortable, it's okay to politely walk away or seek a more populated area.

Ultimately, Puerto Rico is a great destination for women traveling alone, as long as they stay alert, stick to well-traveled areas, and use common sense. The island offers incredible experiences, from exploring historic sites to enjoying pristine beaches, and with a bit of preparation and awareness, solo women travelers can have a safe and memorable adventure.

 For more personal insights on traveling solo in Puerto Rico, please visit **https://www.girlabouttheglobe.com/solo-travel-in-puerto-rico/**.

## Traveling as a Family

Traveling to Puerto Rico as a family can be an unforgettable experience, filled with adventure, culture, and stunning landscapes. However, like any travel destination, it's important to take some safety and health precautions when traveling with children to ensure a smooth and enjoyable trip. Fortunately, Puerto Rico is a **family-friendly destination**, but there are a few things to keep in mind to protect your little ones during your stay.

First, **be aware of the weather**. Puerto Rico's tropical climate means that it's warm year-round, with the summer months often reaching **high humidity** and **temperatures**. When traveling with kids, it's crucial to keep them hydrated, wear sunscreen, and dress in lightweight, breathable clothing. Make sure to apply sunscreen frequently, especially during outdoor activities like beach outings or hikes, as the sun can be intense. Hats, sunglasses, and protective clothing can also provide additional protection against the sun.

If you plan to spend time at the beach, remember that some areas can have **strong waves**, so always supervise your children closely when near the water. While beaches like **Isla Verde** and **Condado** are often calmer and family-friendly, others, such as **Crash Boat Beach** in Aguadilla, can have more powerful surf. Be sure to **check the water conditions** before you go swimming, and if in doubt, stick to swimming pools where lifeguards are on duty.

When it comes to **health precautions**, Puerto Rico is a U.S. territory, so there's no need for special vaccinations or health considerations beyond those you would typically need when traveling within the United States. However, you may want to bring any necessary medications for your children, as some specific brands or prescriptions may not be readily available. It's also wise to carry a basic first-aid kit, especially if you plan on hiking or exploring remote areas where medical services might be farther away. In case of a medical emergency, hospitals like **Puerto Rico Medical Center** in San Juan provide excellent care, but it's always a good idea to know the location of nearby clinics or pharmacies.

If your children suffer from food allergies, it's important to **be cautious about local cuisine**. Puerto Rican food is delicious, but it's often rich in spices, seafood, and tropical fruits. Always ask about ingredients when dining out to avoid any allergic reactions. Many restaurants in tourist areas will be more than happy to accommodate special dietary needs if informed in advance. If your child has severe allergies, you might want to bring along a translation card that explains their dietary restrictions in Spanish.

For general safety when traveling with kids, avoid the more crowded or less-developed areas after dark. While Puerto Rico is a generally safe destination, it's best to stick to well-lit, busy areas in cities like Old San Juan or Condado when out after nightfall. It's also a good idea to keep an eye on your belongings, especially in bustling areas or markets where pickpocketing can happen.

Another consideration is **transportation**. While public transportation exists in Puerto Rico, many families opt to rent a car for flexibility and convenience. Ensure that your rental car is equipped with appropriate **child safety seats**. If you plan to rely on taxis or rideshares, make sure that car seats are available, as not all vehicles will be equipped with them.

Lastly, remember that while Puerto Rico is a U.S. territory, there are some differences from the mainland. For example, tap water is generally safe to drink in most parts of Puerto Rico, but it's always a good idea to double-check, especially if you're staying in rural or less developed areas. Keep bottled water on hand just in case.

## Advice for All Travelers

When traveling to Puerto Rico, it's important to stay aware and prepared to ensure a safe and enjoyable trip. While the island is generally safe and welcoming, there are a few things all travelers—whether solo, with family, or in a group—should be cautious about to avoid potential pitfalls:

- **Watch Your Belongings in Crowded Areas:** Puerto Rico, like many tourist destinations, has its share of petty crime. Be cautious of pickpocketing, especially in crowded areas and popular beaches. Keep an eye on your belongings and consider using anti-theft bags or money belts.

- **Stay Aware of Local Traffic:** Traffic can be chaotic, especially in San Juan. Drivers may not always follow the rules, and pedestrians should be extra cautious. If renting a car, be aware of road conditions, especially in rural areas. In taxis or rideshares, check your route to ensure you're headed the right way.

- **Prepare for Sudden Weather Changes:** Puerto Rico's tropical climate means afternoon rain showers are common. Always carry an umbrella or rain jacket, and check weather forecasts before outdoor activities. Stay alert to potential storms, particularly during the rainy season (May to November).

- **Know Local Emergency Services:** In case of an emergency, dial 911 for police, fire, or medical help. However, if traveling to more remote areas, familiarize yourself with local medical facilities and clinics, as services may be farther away.

- **Don't Drink the Tap Water Everywhere:** Most tap water in Puerto Rico is safe to drink, but in some rural areas, it's better to buy bottled water. If you're unsure, ask locals or hotel staff about the water quality.

- **Avoid Unofficial Beaches or Remote Areas After Dark:** Some secluded beaches or isolated areas can be unsafe after dark. Stick to well-lit, populated areas in the evening for your own safety.

- **Respect Local Customs and Environment:** Puerto Ricans take pride in their culture. Greet locals with a friendly "hola" or "buenos días," and respect the environment by not leaving trash behind, especially on beaches.

- **Be Cautious with Alcohol and Nightlife:** Puerto Rico's nightlife is lively but be cautious with alcohol. Don't leave drinks unattended, and use rideshare services carefully by double-checking car details before getting in.

- **Beware of Scams:** Be cautious of common scams targeting tourists. Always research and book tours through reputable companies and avoid offers that seem too good to be true.

- **Hurricane Season Awareness:** During hurricane season (June-November), stay updated on weather forecasts and have a basic emergency kit ready. Follow any advisories from local authorities.

By staying cautious and informed, you can enjoy Puerto Rico's stunning landscapes, rich culture, and warm hospitality while ensuring a safe and enjoyable experience.

 ## Do's and Don'ts While in Puerto Rico

When visiting Puerto Rico, understanding and respecting the local culture can make your experience more enjoyable and rewarding. Like any destination, Puerto Rico has its own set of customs and social norms that may differ from what you're used to. By following a few simple do's and don'ts, you'll not only ensure a smoother trip but also show respect for the island's rich heritage and traditions. Here's a quick guide to help you navigate Puerto Rican culture with ease and confidence:

- **Do** respect the local culture. Puerto Ricans take pride in their traditions. Greet locals with a friendly "hola" or "buenos días," and show appreciation for their customs.

- **Don't** leave your valuables unattended. Petty theft can happen in crowded areas, so always keep an eye on your belongings, especially in tourist spots.

- **Do** try local foods. Puerto Rican cuisine is a highlight. Don't miss dishes like *mofongo, arroz con gandules,* and *lechón.*

- **Don't** ignore traffic rules. Puerto Rican driving can be chaotic, so always be cautious, especially when crossing streets or renting a car.

- **Do** support local businesses. Shop for handmade goods, eat at local restaurants, and stay in locally-owned accommodations to support the island's economy.

- **Don't** assume everyone speaks English. While many Puerto Ricans are bilingual, especially in tourist areas, Spanish is the island's primary language. Learning a few basic Spanish phrases will show respect and can enhance your experience.

- **Do** greet people warmly. A handshake or cheek kiss (on both cheeks) is common when meeting someone. It's a sign of friendliness and respect, especially in social or family settings.

- **Don't** tip inappropriately. While tipping is customary, it's important to note that 15-20 percent is standard in restaurants. Be mindful that some restaurants may already include a service charge in the bill, especially in tourist areas.

- **Do** dress modestly when visiting churches or religious sites. While Puerto Rico is generally laid-back about clothing, when visiting places of worship, it's respectful to cover shoulders and avoid overly revealing clothing.

- **Don't** bring up sensitive political topics unless you're invited. Puerto Rico's political status (whether it should remain a U.S. territory, become a state, or gain independence) is a sensitive subject for many locals. If you're not familiar with the topic, it's best to avoid discussing it unless the other person brings it up.

CHAPTER 22

# TOURIST TAXATION

## IN THIS CHAPTER

- Overview
- Tourist Taxes in Puerto Rico
- Law of the Land Hypothetical

# TOURIST TAXATION

## Overview

**Tourism** plays a vital role in Puerto Rico's broader economic framework, contributing significantly to the island's GDP and job market. As **one of the top industries in Puerto Rico,** tourism generates billions of dollars annually. It supports a wide range of businesses, from hotels and restaurants to transportation services and local attractions. Thousands of people are employed in tourism-related sectors, making it an essential engine for economic growth and job creation, particularly in popular areas like San Juan, Vieques, and Ponce.

**Tourists** are required to pay **taxes** in Puerto Rico primarily to **help fund public services and infrastructure** that support the tourism industry and the broader community. These taxes, including the **tourist tax** or **room tax** on accommodations, as well as sales taxes on purchases, are a direct way for visitors to contribute to the upkeep and development of the island. Since Puerto Rico, as a U.S. territory, does not have the same level of federal funding as a state, tourism taxes play an important role in helping maintain local resources and services that benefit both residents and visitors.

These tourist taxes are used to improve infrastructure like roads, public transportation, and airports, which directly impact the travel experience and overall quality of life. They also support essential public services, such as healthcare, education, and law enforcement, ensuring that the island can continue to provide a safe and pleasant environment for tourists while sustaining the local economy. Additionally, some of the funds are used for marketing and tourism promotion to attract more visitors, creating a continuous cycle that boosts the economy.

## Tourist Taxes in Puerto Rico

In Puerto Rico, there are several types of tourist-related taxes that visitors should be aware of. These taxes are levied by the local government to help fund the territory's tourism infrastructure and services. Here's a breakdown of the key tourist taxes in Puerto Rico, how they're calculated, and how they contribute to the island's economy:

1. **Room Tax (Hotel Occupancy Tax):** The hotel occupancy tax is typically 7 percent of the room rate. This tax is calculated based on the total cost of the room, including any service charges or resort fees. The tax is generally paid by the guest staying at the hotel, guesthouse, or vacation rental. The hotel or accommodation provider will collect this tax from the guest at the time of booking or check-out and remit it to the Puerto Rican government.

2. **Sales Tax (IVU - Impuesto sobre Ventas y Uso):** The general sales tax in Puerto Rico is 11.5 percent, which is made up of 10.5 percent for the state and 1 percent for local municipalities. This sales tax applies to goods and services, including most purchases made by tourists (e.g., food, shopping, excursions, car rentals). Tourists pay this tax when they make purchases from businesses operating in Puerto Rico. The tax is typically included in the price of the item or service, and the business collects and remits it to the government.

3. **Airport Departure Tax (Tourist Departure Tax):** There is an US$18 airport departure tax for passengers flying out of Puerto Rico. This tax is a flat fee per passenger on outbound flights. Travelers leaving Puerto Rico via an international flight are responsible for paying this fee. The Departure Tax is typically included in the price of the airline ticket, so passengers don't need to pay it separately at the airport.

4. **Cruise Passenger Tax:** Cruise passengers who embark or disembark in Puerto Rico are subject to a US$5-$10 port fee, depending on the specific cruise line or port regulations. This fee is generally a flat charge per passenger aboard cruises arriving at or departing from Puerto Rico's ports. The fee is generally included in the cruise package price or collected by the cruise line at the time of booking.

5. **Car Rental Tax:** There is a US$2 per day tax on car rentals in Puerto Rico, in addition to the regular sales tax. This tax is charged per rental day, paid by the renter of the vehicle. The car rental agency collects the tax and remits it to the Puerto Rican government at the time of rental.

Some municipalities in Puerto Rico may have additional taxes, or the rates could vary slightly depending on the location (e.g., San Juan versus rural areas). Most of these taxes are collected directly by the businesses (hotels, restaurants, car rental agencies, etc.) that tourists interact with during their stay, so tourists typically don't need to worry about making separate payments for these taxes.

 **Law of the Land Hypothetical**

**HYPOTHETICAL**: *David is staying at a hotel in Puerto Rico for a few days. He notices on his booking confirmation that a "7% room tax" is mentioned. When checking in, he asks the receptionist if this tax is mandatory. He also wonders if there are any other taxes he should expect to pay during his visit.*

**ANSWER**: ***Yes.*** *The 7% room tax is indeed mandatory in Puerto Rico. It applies to all hotel stays and is collected by the hotel, helping to fund the island's tourism infrastructure. In addition to this, David should expect to pay the local sales tax of 11.5% on most purchases, such as food, souvenirs, and activities. If he rents a car, there will be an additional US$2 per day car rental tax. These taxes are standard for all visitors to Puerto Rico and contribute to maintaining the island's tourism facilities and services.*

# LONG-TERM STAYS

CHAPTER 23

# LONG-TERM STAYS

## Overview

Many people choose to stay long-term in Puerto Rico for its unique blend of American convenience and Caribbean charm. The island's stunning beaches, rich history, and vibrant cultural scene make it an attractive destination for expats, retirees, and digital nomads. Puerto Rico offers a diverse environment, from bustling urban life in San Juan to the tranquil countryside of the island's interior. **It's an ideal choice for those looking to experience tropical living while still enjoying access to U.S. services and infrastructure.** The island's friendly locals, warm climate year-round, and relaxed pace of life contribute to its appeal. Additionally, Puerto Rico offers **various tax incentives** for U.S. citizens and retirees, making it a popular spot for those seeking tax relief or new opportunities.

With an **established expat community** in places like San Juan, Dorado, and Ponce, newcomers can quickly adapt to life on the island. The island offers a **high standard of living**, with modern amenities like healthcare and reliable internet access, all set against a backdrop of beautiful landscapes. While some areas face challenges with crime and infrastructure, many of the expat-friendly neighborhoods offer a safe, comfortable environment to call home. Puerto Rico also offers the benefit of being part of the U.S., which makes it easier for U.S. citizens to relocate without the need for visas, making the transition smoother than many international moves.

Puerto Rico has something for everyone, whether you're looking for a fast-paced urban lifestyle or a quiet retreat. **San Juan**, the capital, is perfect for those seeking modern amenities, cultural events, and career opportunities. It's the economic and cultural heart of Puerto Rico, offering everything from upscale shopping to vibrant nightlife. If you prefer a mix of city access with a more laid-back atmosphere, neighborhoods like **Condado** or **Isla Verde** are great options, providing easy access to San Juan while offering beautiful beaches and a resort-like lifestyle.

For those looking for a slower pace, places like **Vieques** and **Culebra** offer remote island living with pristine beaches and a relaxed environment. The smaller towns of **Ponce** and **Rincón** are also popular with retirees, surfers, and those seeking a more serene lifestyle away from the tourist crowds. Rincón is particularly known for its surfing culture, while Ponce offers historical charm and a sense of Puerto Rico's cultural heritage.

If you love nature, areas near El Yunque National Forest, like **Luquillo**, offer lush rainforests, waterfalls, and a peaceful atmosphere. In contrast, if you're drawn to mountains and cooler temperatures, towns like **Jayuya** and **Adjuntas** are nestled in the central highlands, providing a cooler climate and rural living options.

*Living Costs in Puerto Rico*

Living in Puerto Rico can be surprisingly **affordable**, especially when compared to mainland U.S. cities, though costs may vary depending on the region. **Housing** is one of the most significant savings for expats, with rental prices in San Juan typically ranging from **US$800 to $1,500 per month** for a one-bedroom apartment in a good area. In more rural areas, rents can be as low as US$500–$700 per month for similar accommodations. Luxury homes or apartments can be found in upscale neighborhoods for higher prices, but overall, housing is **more affordable than in major U.S. cities.**

**Utilities**, including electricity, water, and internet, average about **US$150–$250 per month**, though this can fluctuate based on location and usage. **Groceries** in Puerto Rico are **more expensive than on the U.S. mainland** due to the island's reliance on imports, with a monthly grocery bill averaging **US$300–$400 for a single person**. **Dining out** is relatively affordable, with a meal at a mid-range restaurant costing between **US$12–$20 per person**. Public transportation is minimal on the island, so most residents rely on cars, with gas prices fluctuating around US$4–$5 per gallon.

## Housing Options for Long-Term Stays

Puerto Rico offers a wide **variety of housing options**, from modern apartments in urban areas to rustic homes in the countryside. In San Juan, you'll find everything from luxury condos in the Condado district to more affordable apartments in residential neighborhoods like Río Piedras. In smaller towns or rural areas, houses with large yards and breathtaking views of the island's mountains and beaches are common. Popular areas like Dorado and Ponce offer a mix of upscale homes and more modest rental options, catering to a range of budgets.

If you're looking for more isolated living, areas like Vieques or Culebra offer beachfront cottages or homes in quieter settings. Gated communities are also common in expat-friendly areas, providing added security and amenities like community pools and gyms. For those seeking a traditional Caribbean-style home, you can find colorful houses with verandas in towns like Ponce, Mayagüez, or Bayamón.

## Transportation Options

Puerto Rico has a relatively **limited public transportation system**, mainly concentrated in San Juan, with **buses** being the **primary method of transit**. However, the bus system can be slow and inconsistent, so most long-term residents opt to rent or own cars. **Rental cars** are **widely available** and relatively affordable, but driving can be challenging in certain areas due to narrow streets or mountainous terrain. Taxis are also available, but they tend to be more expensive than renting a car. Ride-sharing services like Uber are popular in San Juan and other urban areas, offering a convenient and affordable alternative to taxis.

For those who prefer to bike, Puerto Rico offers many scenic routes, especially in beach towns like Rincón, where biking is a popular activity. In more rural areas, the limited transportation infrastructure may require owning a car for easier access to essentials and amenities.

## Healthcare Options for Long-Term Visitors

Puerto Rico's healthcare system is of **high quality**, with both **public** and **private options** available to residents. Public healthcare, provided through the Puerto Rico Health Insurance Administration (ASES), is available to all residents, including expats. This system is low-cost but may involve longer wait times for non-urgent services.

Private healthcare in Puerto Rico is excellent, with many hospitals and clinics offering state-of-the-art facilities. Major hospitals in San Juan, such as the Pavia and Ashford hospitals, are well-regarded and provide a wide range of services. **Private healthcare** is often **preferred by expats** for its faster service and personalized care, though it can be more expensive than public healthcare.

For those interested in private health insurance, **international plans are available**, providing coverage for more specialized care and additional services. Overall, healthcare in Puerto Rico is more affordable than in the mainland U.S., making it an attractive option for long-term residents.

## Language Considerations

While English is widely spoken, particularly in tourist areas and larger cities, **learning basic Spanish can be highly beneficial for long-term residents**. Many Puerto Ricans are bilingual, and English is commonly used in business and government settings, but speaking Spanish will make it easier to integrate into local communities, navigate daily life, and establish deeper connections with locals.

Puerto Rican Spanish has its own unique accents and expressions, but it is relatively straightforward, and many newcomers find it easier to learn compared to other Spanish-speaking regions. English is commonly spoken in areas popular with tourists or expats, so communication is not generally an issue in most urban areas.

## Long-Term Visas[61]

The main types of long-term visa options for staying in Puerto Rico are similar to those for the U.S. mainland. For those who wish to live and work in Puerto Rico, it is essential to select the right visa based on employment status, family relationships, or investment plans. Each visa category has specific eligibility requirements, durations, and work restrictions, so it is crucial to consult an immigration lawyer or expert to determine the best option for your situation. Here are the main categories of long-term visas for Puerto Rico:

### 1. Tourist Visa (B-2)

The Tourist Visa is primarily for those visiting Puerto Rico for tourism or leisure purposes. While it can allow stays of up to six months, this visa is not intended for long-term residency or work. You cannot engage in any employment while on a B-2 visa.

- **Duration:** 3–6 months, extendable in some cases.
- **Purpose:** Tourism, visiting family, or medical treatment.
- **Work:** Not permitted.
- **Eligibility:** Must prove non-immigrant intent and demonstrate sufficient financial support for the stay.

### 2. Work Visas

For those who wish to live in Puerto Rico and work, the following work visas are the main options:

- **H-1B Visa (Specialty Occupation Workers):** For individuals in specialized professions requiring a bachelor's degree or higher. A U.S. employer must sponsor the applicant.

---

61  https://christiesrealestatepr.com/blog/
    visa-requirements-moving-puerto-rico

- **L-1 Visa (Intracompany Transferees)**: For employees of multinational companies being transferred to a U.S. office in Puerto Rico. Available for managers, executives, and specialized knowledge workers.

- **O-1 Visa (Individuals with Extraordinary Ability)**: For individuals who have demonstrated extraordinary abilities in their field, such as science, arts, education, or business.

  - **Duration:** Varies by visa type. H-1B allows a stay of up to 3 years, L-1 can be up to 5-7 years, and O-1 can be up to 3 years.

  - **Work:** Permitted, but specific to the sponsoring employer or the type of visa.

### 3. Investor Visa (E-2 Treaty Investor)

The E-2 Treaty Investor Visa is for individuals from countries that have a commerce and navigation treaty with the U.S., who wish to invest a substantial amount of capital in a U.S. business in Puerto Rico.

- **Duration:** Typically 2 years but can be extended indefinitely as long as the business is operational.

- **Work:** Allowed for the investor in their own business.

- **Eligibility:** Must show that the investment is substantial and actively involved in the business.

### 4. Student Visa (F-1)

The F-1 Student Visa is for individuals who wish to study at an accredited U.S. educational institution in Puerto Rico, including universities, colleges, and language programs.

- **Duration:** Valid for the duration of the academic program, with a 60-day grace period after completion.

- **Work:** Part-time on-campus work allowed during school terms; off-campus work is possible with authorization (e.g., Optional Practical Training, or OPT).

- **Eligibility:** Must be accepted into an accredited school and prove financial ability to support oneself.

## 5. Family-Based Immigrant Visas

Family-based visas are available for those who have close family members who are U.S. citizens or lawful permanent residents (Green Card holders) living in Puerto Rico.

- **Immediate Relative Visas (IR):** Available for spouses, unmarried children under 21, and parents of U.S. citizens. This is the fastest and most direct pathway to permanent residence in Puerto Rico.
- **Family Preference Visas:** For other family members, such as adult children or siblings of U.S. citizens, or spouses and children of permanent residents. These visas have annual caps and can involve longer wait times.

    - **Duration:** Typically leads to permanent residency (Green Card).
    - **Work:** Permanent residents are authorized to work.
    - **Eligibility:** A qualifying family relationship must exist, and there may be a waiting period depending on the preference category.

## 6. Retiree Visa/Tax Incentives (Act 60/Former Act 22)

While Puerto Rico does not offer a specific "retirement visa," Act 60 (formerly Acts 20 and 22) offers significant tax incentives for U.S. citizens (and residents) who relocate to Puerto Rico and become bona fide residents. These incentives can significantly reduce taxes on income, capital gains, and dividends.

- **Duration:** No fixed time limit for tax benefits as long as residency requirements are met.
- **Work:** Individuals who qualify for Act 60 typically do not need to work; however, those who invest in Puerto Rican businesses or engage in business activities can benefit from tax incentives.

- **Eligibility:** Must meet residency requirements (usually spending at least 183 days per year in Puerto Rico and proving intent to live there permanently).

### 7. *Humanitarian Visas (Asylum)*

Individuals who face persecution in their home country can apply for asylum in Puerto Rico under U.S. law. This would allow them to stay in Puerto Rico while their asylum claim is processed.

- **Duration:** Asylum is typically granted for an indefinite period, though the applicant must renew their status periodically.
- **Work:** Authorized after 180 days if asylum has not been adjudicated.
- **Eligibility:** Must demonstrate a well-founded fear of persecution due to race, religion, nationality, political opinion, or membership in a social group.

 **General Questions**

1. *If I want to stay in Puerto Rico for long-term and work, should I apply for a work permit before arriving in Puerto Rico?*
   **Yes.** If you're not a U.S. citizen or Green Card holder and want to work in Puerto Rico, you must apply for a work visa (e.g., H-1B, L-1, O-1) before arriving. You cannot switch from a tourist visa to a work visa while in Puerto Rico. U.S. citizens do not need a work permit.

2. *I am American. Can I retire to Puerto Rico?* **Yes.** U.S. citizens can retire to Puerto Rico without a visa. If you want to benefit from tax incentives under Act 60 (e.g., reduced taxes on investments), you need to establish bona fide residency, which requires spending at least 183 days per year in Puerto Rico.

 **Law of the Land Hypothetical**

**HYPOTHETICAL**: *John, a software developer from Canada, wants to move to Puerto Rico to work remotely for his U.S.-based company. He's interested in the tax incentives available for individuals relocating to the island but isn't sure about his visa requirements. Does John need a work visa to live and work remotely in Puerto Rico, and how can he take advantage of tax incentives?*

**ANSWER**: *Since John is not a U.S. citizen or Green Card holder, he needs to apply for an appropriate visa, such as the B-2 tourist visa for initial entry or the E-2 investor visa if he plans to establish a business in Puerto Rico. However, if John is working remotely for a U.S.-based company and not engaging in local employment, he may be able to live in Puerto Rico under a tourist visa, as long as he doesn't violate any work restrictions. To benefit from tax incentives under Act 60, John would need to establish bona fide residency by spending at least 183 days a year in Puerto Rico and proving his intent to live there permanently. Consulting with a visa and tax expert is recommended to ensure compliance with all immigration and tax laws.*

 **Takeaways**

- Puerto Rico offers a distinctive lifestyle, combining American infrastructure and services with Caribbean charm. Expats, retirees, and digital nomads are drawn to the island's warm climate, relaxed pace, vibrant culture, and tax incentives, making it a popular long-term destination for those looking for tropical living with access to U.S. benefits.

- While living costs can vary across the island, Puerto Rico offers more affordable housing compared to mainland U.S. cities, particularly in rural areas. However, groceries and dining out can be more expensive due to the island's reliance on imports.

- Puerto Rico provides a wide range of housing options, from luxury condos in urban areas like San Juan to tranquil homes in rural areas or smaller towns. For those seeking a slower pace, places like Vieques, Culebra, and Rincón offer remote living and access to stunning beaches and natural beauty.

- The public transportation system is limited, especially outside San Juan, so owning a car is often necessary. Rentable cars, taxis, and ride-sharing services like Uber are commonly used, and biking is a popular activity in coastal towns like Rincón.

- U.S. citizens can relocate to Puerto Rico without a visa, but those looking to take advantage of tax benefits must meet residency requirements, including spending at least 183 days on the island. Non-U.S. citizens will need to apply for appropriate visas, such as work, investor, or student visas, depending on their circumstances.

# CHAPTER 24
# CIVIL LITIGATION

# CIVIL LITIGATION

## Overview

Civil litigation provides a mechanism for resolving disputes, ensuring that travelers have a way to seek justice if legal issues arise while visiting another country. It helps them understand their rights and obligations under local laws, which may differ from those in their home country. The civil litigation system offers a formal process for addressing conflicts, such as contract disputes or personal injury claims, and can deter unfair practices by encouraging businesses to comply with legal standards. It also allows individuals to seek financial recourse for damages or losses and helps protect them from potential exploitation by local entities. Overall, understanding civil litigation enhances a visitor's experience and safety while traveling.

## Personal Injury Claims and Compensation Law

To establish a **valid personal injury claim** in Puerto Rico, the claimant must prove that the following four elements exist: **duty of care**, **breach of duty**, **causation**, and **damages**. **Duty of care** refers to the legal obligation that one party has to ensure the safety and well-being of others. For example, drivers have a duty to adhere to traffic laws and drive safely, which establishes a standard of care owed to other road users and pedestrians.

**Breach of duty** occurs when an individual or entity fails to meet this standard of care, leading to negligent actions. An example is a driver who causes an accident by texting while driving. The claimant must then demonstrate that the breach of duty directly caused their injuries, a requirement known as causation. This means the plaintiff must show a clear link between the defendant's actions and the injuries sustained.

Finally, **damages** represent the losses incurred by the injured party, which can include medical expenses, lost wages, and pain and suffering. In Puerto Rico, the injured party can seek compensation for both economic and non-economic damages.

When an individual suffers an injury due to someone else's fault or negligence, there are **essential steps to follow** to protect their rights and support any eventual legal claims. First and foremost, **seeking medical treatment** is vital, as it ensures that injuries are treated and documented officially, which is crucial for any claims. In addition to medical records, taking photographs of the accident scene and obtaining witness contact information can serve as critical evidence later.

The injured party should **report the incident** to the relevant authorities, such as the police or hospital administrators. A police report can provide an official account of the incident and serve as supporting evidence in legal proceedings. It is important not to admit fault or make any incriminating statements at the scene, as these could complicate the legal process later on.

After addressing immediate medical and safety needs, **consulting with a personal injury attorney is advisable.** An experienced attorney can help assess the claim's merits, navigate the complexities of local laws, and work toward achieving a fair settlement.

### *How Are Damages Calculated?*

In Puerto Rico, damages in personal injury cases can be broadly categorized into economic and non-economic damages. **Economic damages** are quantifiable losses with established monetary values, including medical expenses, rehabilitation costs, lost wages, and other out-of-pocket expenses directly related to the injury.[62]

**Non-economic damages** are more subjective and include **compensation for pain and suffering, emotional distress, loss of enjoyment of life**, and **any other intangible losses**. While these damages do not have a clear numeric value, courts often consider the severity of the injury, the duration of recovery, and the overall impact on the victim's quality of life when determining an appropriate amount. Calculating non-economic damages often relies on legal precedents and comparative analyses from similar cases to ensure a fair outcome.[63]

*Role of Insurance*

Insurance plays a significant role in personal injury claims in Puerto Rico. Most individuals affected by an accident will turn to the at-fault party's insurance company as part of the claims process. Puerto Rico has a **no-fault insurance system**, which requires drivers to maintain basic insurance that covers medical expenses and lost wages, regardless of who caused the accident.

Upon filing a claim with the insurance company, it is crucial to understand that the insurer aims to minimize payouts. Engaging an attorney can be beneficial in navigating negotiations with insurance adjusters to ensure fair compensation. Insurance policies can be complex, and a lawyer's expertise can help the victim interpret the terms of their coverage and advocate for their rights during negotiations.

*Related Legal Fees*

Legal fees in personal injury cases in Puerto Rico often operate on a **contingency fee basis**. This means that the attorney earns a fee only if the case is successfully resolved, either through a settlement or a court judgment. Contingency fees typically range from **30 percent to 40 percent**

---

62  https://en.olmedolawpsc.com/services/personal-injury/

63  https://www.ragflaw.com/services/personal-injury-law.html

of the total recovery amount, depending on the case's complexity and whether it proceeds to trial.

Additionally, clients should be aware of potential costs related to filing fees, medical record retrieval, investigative services, and expert witness expenses. These costs may be deducted from the final recovery amount or could be billed separately, depending on the attorney's retainer agreement. Thus, it is essential for clients to understand all potential costs involved upfront to avoid unexpected financial burdens during their recovery process.

## How to File a Civil Claim[64]

Before filing, it's important to ensure that you meet certain requirements. The Puerto Rico court must have jurisdiction over your case, which generally means your claim needs to fall under the court's authority, such as the Superior Court of Puerto Rico. You must also have a valid legal reason for your claim—known as a "cause of action"—and you must be directly affected by the issue you're bringing to court, meaning you have the legal standing to file. Another critical factor to consider is the statute of limitations, as each type of claim has a specific deadline for filing. For example, personal injury claims in Puerto Rico must be filed within one year of the incident.

The types of civil claims you can file are varied. These include breaches of contract, disputes over property, personal injury cases stemming from accidents, family law matters such as divorce and child custody, as well as employment-related issues like wrongful termination or wage disputes. Debt collection is also a common reason for filing a civil claim. Whatever the nature of the case, each type of claim will require its own set of evidence and legal considerations.

When you're ready to file, there are a few key documents you'll need. The first is the complaint (or *demanda*), which outlines the facts and legal basis for your claim. This document should provide a detailed

---

64  https://undisputedlegal.com/puerto-rico-rules-of-civil-procedure/

explanation of the issue, the parties involved, and what kind of reme-dy you're seeking from the court. Along with the complaint, you must submit a **summons** (*citación*), which is a legal notice to the defendant that a lawsuit has been filed against them. The defendant will be given the opportunity to respond within a certain time frame. You will also need to gather and submit any **evidence** supporting your case. This could include contracts, emails, photographs, or witness statements. If you're hiring a lawyer to represent you, a **power of attorney** may also be necessary.

Once all documents are ready, you'll need to **file** them **with the appropriate court**. In Puerto Rico, **civil claims are typically filed in the Superior Court** (*Tribunal Superior*), which is divided into judicial districts. You must file your claim in the district where the defendant lives, where the event occurred, or where the disputed property is located. For instance, if the defendant lives in San Juan, you'd file your claim in the San Juan Judicial District. To file, you'll visit the courthouse in the appropriate district, submit your complaint and supporting documents to the clerk, and pay a filing fee, which varies depending on the nature of the claim. The court clerk will then issue a summons, which will need to be served to the defendant. This service is crucial, as it formally notifies the defendant of the lawsuit.

Though it's possible to file a claim on your own (known as *pro se* representation), it's generally advisable to hire an attorney, especially given the complexity of legal procedures. **The courts in Puerto Rico conduct proceedings in Spanish, so you'll need to ensure that all your filings are in the language unless special arrangements are made for translation.**

## Service of Documents

The service of documents in Puerto Rico is regulated by the **Puerto Rico Rules of Civil Procedure** (RPCP), which are based on the **Federal Rules of Civil Procedure** but tailored to Puerto Rico's legal framework. The most relevant sections are **Rule 4** of the Puerto Rico Rules of Civil Procedure, which defines service of process, the **Puerto Rico Civil Code**, and **specific local statutes** for certain types of cases (family law, labor law, etc.), and may also contain specialized rules for service.

In Puerto Rico, legal documents can be served in several ways. The most common method is **personal service**, where the documents are directly delivered to the defendant by a sheriff or an authorized process server. If personal service is not possible, documents can be sent by **certified mail with a return receipt** requested to ensure the recipient acknowledges receipt. When personal service can't be made, substitute service is used, where documents may be delivered to a family member or another person at the defendant's home, provided they are of a certain age and the location is within the same municipality. If the defendant's location is unknown, service can be made **through publication in a local newspaper**, but only with court authorization. For corporations or legal entities, documents are served by an officer, managing agent, or registered agent, or alternatively, they can be mailed to the entity's last known address.

## Statute of Limitations

In Puerto Rico, the statute of limitations for civil suits is primarily governed by the Civil Code, which outlines the time periods within which different types of claims must be filed. The general **statute of limitations for most civil actions is 15 years**, meaning that if you wish to file a lawsuit based on a civil matter, you generally have 15 years to do so. However, certain claims are subject to different timeframes. For instance, claims related to **written contracts** must be filed within **15 years**, while **oral contract** claims must be initiated within **6 years**. **Tort claims**, such as personal injury cases, have a much shorter limitation period of only **1 year** from the date the injury occurred. Similarly, claims involving **fraud** must also be filed within **one year**, but the clock starts from the moment the fraud is discovered, rather than when it occurred.

Several factors can affect the length of the statute of limitations. For example, the nature of the claim itself plays a significant role, as does the relationship between the parties involved. Additionally, in some cases, specific circumstances may toll or delay the statute of limitations. For instance, if the injured party is a minor, mentally incapacitated, or otherwise unable to file a claim, the limitation period may be extended. Similarly, if the defendant is absent from the jurisdiction, the statute of limitations may be paused until they return.

If a civil suit is filed after the statute of limitations has expired, the court will typically dismiss the case, as the defendant can raise the expiration of the limitations period as a defense. However, there are exceptions to this rule. One notable exception is the "discovery rule," which allows the statute of limitations to be extended in cases where the injury or harm was not immediately apparent, such as in cases of medical malpractice or fraud. In these instances, the clock starts ticking not from the date of the act or injury, but from when the plaintiff discovered, or should have reasonably discovered, the harm.

These time limitations and exceptions are critical for anyone considering legal action in Puerto Rico, as failing to file a claim within the prescribed time can result in the loss of the right to seek a remedy.

 ## Getting Married in Puerto Rico

Getting married in Puerto Rico involves a simple legal process, whether you are a resident or a foreign national. The general legal requirements for marriage include both parties being **at least 18 years old**, though minors 16 or 17 can marry with parental consent and court approval. In rare cases, minors under 16 may also marry with court permission. The couple must also be legally competent to marry, meaning neither party can be currently married or closely related to one another. **Same-sex marriages** are also **legal** in Puerto Rico, and the laws surrounding marriage apply equally to all couples.

To apply for a marriage license in Puerto Rico, both individuals must present valid identification, such as a passport, birth certificate, or **government-issued ID**. If either party has been previously married, they must provide a certified copy of the divorce decree or the deceased spouse's death certificate. The couple must go to the Civil

Registry Office (*Registro Demográfico*) in the municipality where they plan to marry and complete a **marriage license application**. The fee for the license is typically **around US$150**, though it may vary slightly depending on the municipality. Once the application and payment are submitted, the license is usually issued on the same day or within 1 to 2 days, assuming all documentation is in order.

There are **no residency requirements** for foreign nationals wishing to marry in Puerto Rico. Non-residents can marry there just as easily as residents. However, the **documents must either be in Spanish or accompanied by certified translations.** The application process for non-residents is the same, and they must appear in person to submit their documents and pay the fee at the Civil Registry Office.

For the marriage ceremony, couples can choose between a civil ceremony and a religious ceremony. A **civil ceremony** is typically conducted by a judge, notary public, or an official from the Civil Registry Office, and it can take place at the registry office or another designated location, such as a courthouse. It is a legal marriage that does not require any religious or ceremonial aspects. On the other hand, a **religious ceremony** can be performed by an ordained clergy member, such as a priest or pastor, but it must be followed by the legal step of obtaining a marriage license from the Civil Registry to be legally recognized. **A religious ceremony alone is not sufficient to establish a legal marriage in Puerto Rico.**

Once the ceremony is performed, whether civil or religious, the officiant will file the marriage certificate with the Civil Registry Office, officially registering the marriage. The couple will then receive a certified marriage certificate, which serves as legal proof of the union. This certificate is necessary for name changes, tax purposes, or any other legal matters requiring proof of marriage.

As Puerto Rico is a U.S. territory, marriages performed there are legally valid in all U.S. states and territories. For foreign nationals, Puerto Rican marriages are **generally recognized internationally**, though it is wise to check with the relevant embassy or consulate for specific requirements in the country where the couple resides.

 **Law of the Land Hypothetical**

**HYPOTHETICAL**: *Olivia, a tourist visiting Puerto Rico, is walking along a sidewalk near the beach in San Juan. She trips over a raised section of the pavement and injures her ankle. After seeking medical attention, it is determined that Olivia's injury requires surgery, and she will be unable to work for several months. As a result, she incurs significant medical expenses and lost wages during her recovery. Olivia wants to pursue a personal injury claim against the municipality of San Juan, arguing that the city is responsible for maintaining safe sidewalks and that the raised pavement was a clear hazard. However, she is unsure about how to proceed with the lawsuit, particularly regarding the statute of limitations and the process for filing her claim in Puerto Rico.*

**ANSWER**: *Maria has one year from the date of her accident to file a personal injury claim in Puerto Rico. To pursue the claim, she should first gather evidence, including medical records, photos of the raised pavement, witness statements, and any relevant police reports. Next, she will need to prepare and file a complaint with the Superior Court of Puerto Rico in San Juan, outlining the facts, legal grounds, and the damages she is seeking. After filing, she must ensure the municipality of San Juan is formally notified through a summons. Maria will also need to pay filing fees and any additional costs for document service or expert witnesses. Lastly, while it is possible to file without legal representation, consulting a local attorney is highly recommended to guide her through the legal process. Given the statute of limitations of one year from the date of the accident, Maria must act promptly to protect her legal rights.*

# OTHER THINGS TO KNOW

## CHAPTER 25

# OTHER THINGS TO KNOW

## Tourists and Street Hustling

Street hustling in Puerto Rico is an issue that, while not overwhelming, remains a **notable concern for many tourists**, particularly in popular tourist areas. While the island is generally safe and welcoming, certain behaviors associated with street hustling can lead to uncomfortable situations for those unfamiliar with local practices. Tourists, often distracted by the island's beauty and culture, may become easy targets for aggressive vendors and scammers looking to make a quick profit. While not pervasive across the entire island, hustling is more **concentrated in specific, high-traffic areas** where visitors are most likely to engage with street vendors and performers.

One of the **most common scams** tourists encounters is the **"free gift" hustle**. Vendors may approach tourists with small trinkets, flowers, or other items, offering them as "gifts." After the item is handed over, the hustler then demands payment, often for a price much higher than expected. This can create an uncomfortable situation for tourists, especially when they feel pressured to pay for something they didn't ask for. In other cases, street performers may put on a show or play music in a public space, only to demand payment after the performance. If tourists don't want to pay, the hustler can become aggressive, sometimes even following the tourists down the street, making it difficult to escape the situation without confrontation.

**Overcharging** for services is another frequent scam. Tourists may find themselves targeted by taxi drivers who charge exorbitant rates for short rides, taking advantage of visitors who aren't familiar with local prices. Similar situations can occur with beach rentals or guided tours. The price quoted is often lower than what is ultimately charged, or hidden fees appear after the service has already been rendered. These deceptive practices can leave tourists frustrated, especially when they realize they've been scammed after the fact.

The areas most known for street hustling are typically those that attract a large number of tourists. **Old San Juan**, with its narrow cobblestone streets and popular landmarks, is a prime location for vendors looking to sell everything from cheap souvenirs to "authentic" Puerto Rican artwork. As tourists wander through this historic district, they may encounter individuals offering them trinkets or "special deals" on items that aren't what they seem. Similarly, **Condado** and **Isla Verde**, two of Puerto Rico's most visited beach and nightlife destinations, see a high concentration of street hustlers. These areas, filled with tourists enjoying the beaches or heading out to dinner, provide opportunities for hustlers to approach visitors with deals that sound too good to be true. **Rincon**, a smaller surf town, is also not immune to such tactics, with hustlers offering surf lessons or beach rentals at prices that can be much higher than expected.

Local authorities and tourism organizations in Puerto Rico are aware of street hustling and have efforts in place to address it, though **enforcement can be inconsistent**. The Puerto Rico Tourism Company runs campaigns to inform tourists about common scams, offering safety tips through brochures and online resources. These campaigns encourage visitors to be cautious with unsolicited offers, agree on prices upfront, and avoid feeling pressured into purchases or services.

While local police patrol tourist-heavy areas and may intervene if vendors are aggressive or breaking regulations, many street hustlers operate in ways that are hard to regulate. Some vendors have permits, while others work without oversight, leading to limited enforcement. The local business community, including hotels and tour operators, also plays a role by warning tourists about scams and recommending reputable services. Despite these efforts, street hustling remains a persistent issue in popular tourist areas.

## Safety Concerns and Practical Tips

When it comes to interacting with street hustlers in Puerto Rico, several safety concerns can arise, particularly for tourists who may not be familiar with the local environment or the common tactics used by scammers. These interactions can lead to emotional distress, financial loss, and in some cases, even physical altercations if the hustlers become aggressive or refuse to take "no" for an answer.

One of the primary safety concerns is the potential for aggressive behavior from hustlers who feel that they've been rejected or that they haven't made enough money from a tourist. If a hustler offers an item or service and the tourist declines, the situation can sometimes escalate, with the vendor following the person, raising their voice, or becoming confrontational. This can be intimidating, especially in areas with large crowds where it's difficult to quickly escape the interaction. Some hustlers may also try to distract tourists or work in groups, using one person to engage while another attempts to steal personal items like wallets or phones.

Another risk involves tourists being overcharged for goods or services, as many street vendors and hustlers target those unfamiliar with local pricing. Although this may not feel physically dangerous, it can lead to significant financial loss, particularly if tourists are pressured into purchasing overpriced or substandard items or paying for services that weren't agreed upon in advance.

To protect themselves from aggressive hustlers and avoid falling into these common traps, tourists should follow some **basic safety measures**. First and foremost, it's important to **remain calm and assertive**. If a hustler approaches, tourists should politely but firmly say "no" and continue walking away without engaging further. If a situation begins to escalate or a hustler becomes persistent, it's best to move toward a more populated or safer area, where the presence of others can discourage any aggressive behavior. In cases where tourists feel physically threatened, they should not hesitate to seek help from nearby locals or call the police.

Before engaging in any transaction, especially with street vendors, tourists should **agree on a price upfront** to avoid surprises later on. Always ask for the total cost of a service or product before committing to it and ensure that any transactions are done with legitimate businesses. Using ATMs in well-lit, busy areas and **avoiding walking alone at night**, especially in unfamiliar parts of towns, can also help minimize risks.

To stay safe, tourists should remain calm and assertive, say "no" firmly, and walk away if approached. If the situation escalates, they should move to a more populated area and seek help if needed. Tourists should avoid accepting "free" gifts or making deals without agreeing on prices upfront. It's important to only transact with legitimate businesses and use ATMs in busy areas. Understanding local customs, like the common practice of bargaining, can also help navigate interactions safely.

For those who experience harassment or scams, resources are available to report incidents. The Puerto Rico Tourism Company offers a hotline, and local police in tourist areas are equipped to handle complaints. Hotels provide information on how to file reports, and the Department of Consumer Affairs (DACO) can assist with issues like price gouging.

 ## In the Event of Death[65]

If someone traveling with you dies while in Puerto Rico, the situation can be difficult and stressful, but there are clear steps to follow to manage the process in a legal and respectful manner.

---

65  https://wwwnc.cdc.gov/travel/yellowbook/2024/
     environmental-hazards-risks/death-during-travel

The first step is to **immediately contact local authorities**. You should call **911** to report the death, whether it occurred in a hotel, on the street, or elsewhere. If the death happens in a hospital or health facility, the staff will notify the authorities and begin the required formalities. In cases of natural death, the police will issue a death certificate, and in cases of suspicious or unnatural death, such as an accident, a local forensic investigation may be required. A death certificate issued by a licensed doctor in Puerto Rico will be necessary for all further arrangements.

After notifying local authorities, it is essential to **contact your embassy or consulate**.[66] They can assist with a range of services, including coordinating the repatriation of the deceased's body, helping with funeral arrangements, and guiding you through the required paperwork. The embassy can also assist in notifying family members back home and can offer a list of local funeral homes experienced with repatriation services.

When it comes to handling the deceased's remains, if you plan to bring the body back home, the first step is to **contact a local funeral home**. Funeral homes in Puerto Rico can assist with embalming, preparing the body for transportation, and ensuring all legal documents are in order. A **funeral export certificate** must be obtained from the Puerto Rican Department of Health, and the body must be properly embalmed to meet international transportation requirements. The U.S. embassy will issue a **consular mortuary certificate** to facilitate the repatriation process.

Bringing the body home can be costly, and families should prepare for a variety of expenses, including embalming, transportation, caskets, and legal fees for necessary certificates. These costs can range from a few thousand dollars to more, depending on the circumstances. It's important to consult with the embassy and funeral homes about any specific health or transportation requirements, as they may vary depending on the destination country.

---

66 https://travel.state.gov/content/travel/en/international-travel/while-abroad/death-abroad1/return-of-remains-of-deceased-us-citizen.html

## Experiencing Financial Hardship

Experiencing financial hardship while traveling in Puerto Rico is something many tourists may face, often due to **unexpected circumstances.** One of the primary reasons tourists may face financial hardship in Puerto Rico is simply **underestimating the costs of travel.** While Puerto Rico uses the U.S. dollar, some travelers may still find themselves unprepared for the higher prices of food, transportation, and activities, especially in tourist-heavy areas like San Juan, Old San Juan, and Isla Verde.

Another reason can be the unexpected nature of **emergencies.** For example, tourists may face unplanned medical expenses, such as a trip to the hospital due to illness or injury, or costs associated with losing their passport or wallet. Unforeseen travel delays, flight cancellations, or extra nights at accommodations due to transportation issues can also add to the financial strain. Additionally, the temptation to overspend on excursions, souvenirs, and high-end dining can quickly deplete a traveler's budget.

If a tourist runs out of money or needs financial help while in Puerto Rico, the first step is to **contact their bank or credit card company.** Many banks offer emergency cash transfer services and may be able to help you access funds even if your credit or debit card is lost or compromised. Some services, like **Western Union** or **MoneyGram**, can transfer funds from friends or family back home to a local agent in Puerto Rico.

Tourists should also reach out to their **embassy or consulate** for assistance. If you're facing a serious financial emergency, the embassy can offer guidance on accessing emergency funds or direct you to local charitable organizations that may assist in urgent situations.

*Resources and Support Systems for Travelers*

In Puerto Rico, there are several support systems in place for travelers who are struggling financially. The **Puerto Rico Tourism Company** may provide emergency assistance and guide you to reliable financial services.

**Banks** and **ATMs** are widely available, especially in larger cities and tourist areas, and travelers can use international cards to withdraw cash. However, it's important to note that some ATMs may charge a fee for foreign cards.

For those in particularly dire financial situations, local **charities** or community organizations may provide temporary assistance. The **Red Cross of Puerto Rico** and other nonprofit groups may offer resources for tourists in need, such as food, shelter, or transportation.

## *Tips on Budgeting*

To avoid running into financial difficulties, tourists should plan a **realistic budget** before their trip, taking into account daily expenses, emergency funds, and extra costs like souvenirs or activities. Here are some budgeting tips:

- **Set a daily spending limit:** Plan for food, transportation, and activities each day and stick to your limit.
- **Use public transportation:** It's often cheaper than taxis or rental cars, especially in urban areas.
- **Eat like a local:** Puerto Rican street food or small family-run restaurants are usually more affordable and offer authentic cuisine.
- **Book accommodations early:** Avoid high last-minute costs by booking hotels or Airbnbs in advance.
- **Use cash for small transactions:** While credit cards are widely accepted, using cash can help avoid extra fees and make it easier to control spending.
- **Have an emergency plan:** Carry a small amount of cash and a credit card for emergencies and know how to access additional funds if needed.

Understanding local costs, managing your expenses carefully, and knowing where to turn for assistance can help tourists avoid financial hardship and enjoy their trip to Puerto Rico with greater peace of mind.

# QUICK REFERENCE GUIDE

- Quick Chapter References to Important Topics

# QUICK REFERENCE GUIDE

## Crime in Puerto Rico

Are there particular areas I should avoid as a tourist?

While Puerto Rico is generally safe for tourists, areas like **Santurce**, **La Perla** in San Juan, and certain neighborhoods in **Ponce** may have higher crime rates, especially at night. To stay safe, stick to popular areas like **Old San Juan**, **Condado**, and **Isla Verde**, avoid walking alone after dark, and keep your belongings secure. If you feel unsafe, seek a well-lit area, call **911**, or use rideshare services. By staying aware and following basic safety tips, you can enjoy your visit with peace of mind. *For more details, see Chapter 3.*

## Drug Offenses

Is the possession of marijuana legal?

In Puerto Rico, the possession of marijuana is subject to specific regulations. While recreational use remains illegal, **marijuana is legal for medical use** under the Medical Cannabis Act passed in 2015. Patients with a valid prescription can legally use marijuana for certain medical conditions. However, the **recreational use, sale, or possession of marijuana for non-medical purposes is still prohibited**. If a person is caught possessing small amounts, typically less than 6 ounces, they may face fines or other penalties, while larger amounts can lead to more serious consequences, including arrest.

Is the possession of cocaine legal?

**No.** The possession of cocaine is **strictly illegal** in Puerto Rico. Cocaine is classified as a controlled substance, and the law imposes severe penalties for its possession, sale, or use. Regardless of the quantity, being caught with cocaine can result in arrest, hefty fines, and long prison sentences. There is zero tolerance for cocaine-related offenses in Puerto Rico, and the legal consequences are harsh for anyone caught violating these laws. *For more details, see Chapter 4.*

## Alcohol-Related Offenses

What is the legal drinking age?

In Puerto Rico, the legal drinking age is **18 years old**. This applies to the purchase, possession, and consumption of alcoholic beverages. It's important to note that the legal drinking age is consistent with many other regions of the world, and anyone caught supplying alcohol to individuals under 18 can face legal consequences.

What is the legal blood alcohol limit to drive?

The legal blood alcohol limit for drivers in Puerto Rico is **0.08 percent blood alcohol content** (BAC), which is the same as in many U.S. states. Drivers found to have a BAC above this limit can be arrested for driving under the influence (DUI). For commercial drivers or individuals with a history of DUI offenses, the limit may be stricter, and penalties for driving with a high BAC can include fines, license suspension, and even imprisonment. *For more details, see Chapter 5.*

## Firearm & Ammunition Offenses

Can I possess a gun?

**Yes.** It is legal to own a gun in Puerto Rico, but there are several requirements and regulations. To legally possess a firearm, individuals must obtain a **gun license** from the Puerto Rico Police Department. This process includes background checks, fingerprinting, and completing a firearms safety course. Certain firearms, such as automatic weapons, are prohibited for civilian use. Additionally, carrying a firearm in public requires a concealed carry permit, which has its own set of requirements.

Can I possess ammunition?

**Yes.** Possessing ammunition is also legal, but it is subject to the same regulations as firearms. You must have a valid gun license to possess ammunition, and ammunition for restricted firearms, like assault rifles, may have additional restrictions. *For more details, see Chapter 6.*

## Prostitution

Is prostitution legal?

**No.** Prostitution is **illegal** in Puerto Rico. While the act of selling sex is not explicitly criminalized, certain related activities, such as pimping, soliciting, and operating brothels, are prohibited under Puerto Rican law. Engaging in prostitution, or any activities that promote it, can result in legal penalties, including fines and imprisonment. *For more details, see Chapter 7.*

## LGBTQ

Is homosexuality legal?

**Yes. Homosexuality is legal** in Puerto Rico. Same-sex sexual activity has been legal in Puerto Rico since the enactment of the U.S. Supreme Court's Lawrence v. Texas decision in 2003, which decriminalized consensual same-sex activity across the United States, including Puerto Rico.

Are same-sex public displays of affection legal?

**Yes.** Same-sex public displays of affection are also legal in Puerto Rico. The territory has made significant progress in terms of LGBTQ+ rights over the years. Same-sex couples have the right to engage in public displays of affection without legal repercussions. *For more details, see Chapter 8.*

## Arrested in Puerto Rico

Would I be entitled to bail if I'm arrested?

If you're arrested in Puerto Rico, you are generally entitled to bail, unless charged with a serious crime or considered a flight risk. A judge will set the bail amount during an arraignment.

Will a lawyer be provided to me if I cannot afford one?

**Yes.** If you cannot afford a lawyer, a public defender will be appointed to you. This ensures you have legal representation, in line with your right to counsel under U.S. law. *For more details, see Chapter 10.*

## Helping a Friend or Relative Imprisoned in Puerto Rico

Can I send money to a friend or relative imprisoned in Puerto Rico?

**Yes.** You can send money to a friend or family member who is imprisoned in Puerto Rico. Funds can be sent through various methods, such as money orders, electronic transfers, or through services provided by the correctional facility. Typically, inmates can use these funds for commissary purchases, phone calls, and other personal expenses while incarcerated.

Can I remain in Puerto Rico upon release from prison or jail after my sentence is complete?

**Yes.** You can remain in Puerto Rico after completing your sentence, as long as you are a U.S. citizen or legal resident. If you are not a U.S. citizen and are in Puerto Rico on a visa or under a specific immigration status, your ability to remain in Puerto Rico after release will depend on your immigration status and any restrictions placed on you by immigration authorities. *For more details, see Chapter 12.*

## Crime Victim Assistance

Can a victim of a crime be legally compensated?

**Yes.** A victim of a crime in Puerto Rico can be legally compensated through the Puerto Rico Crime Victims Compensation Program. This program offers financial assistance for expenses like medical bills, funeral costs, lost wages, and counseling for victims of violent crimes. Victims must file a claim with the Puerto Rico Department of Justice and meet certain criteria, including cooperating with law enforcement.

Does the Puerto Rican government offer assistance for family members of homicide victims?

**Yes.** Puerto Rico's government does offer assistance. The Crime Victims Compensation Program provides support to the families of homicide victims, including financial aid for funeral expenses, mental health counseling, and other related costs. Additionally, the government may also offer other forms of assistance, such as legal guidance or victim advocacy services, to help families navigate the aftermath of a homicide. *For more details, see Chapter 14.*

## U.S. Consulate Assistance

Are there any limitations to the consulate assistance I can receive while in Puerto Rico?

**Yes.** In Puerto Rico, U.S. citizens typically don't need consular assistance, as the territory falls under U.S. jurisdiction. For foreign nationals, consulates can help with services like lost passports, legal referrals, or repatriation of remains. However, they can't intervene in legal matters under Puerto Rican or U.S. law, provide financial assistance, or cover legal fees. **Assistance is limited by both local and international laws.** *For more details, see Chapter 14.*

## Police

Is there an official police force?

> **Yes.** Puerto Rico has an official police force called the **Puerto Rico Police Department (Policía de Puerto Rico)**. It is a fully operational law enforcement agency responsible for maintaining public order, enforcing laws, and providing security across the territory. *For more details, see Chapter 15.*

## How to Get Legal Help in Puerto Rico

Is there a resource in Puerto Rico to find legal representation?

> **Yes.** There are resources in Puerto Rico to help you find legal representation. The **Puerto Rico Bar Association (Colegio de Abogados y Abogadas de Puerto Rico)** maintains a directory of licensed attorneys who can offer legal services. You can search by practice area or location to find a lawyer who fits your needs.

Is there free legal representation assistance?

> **Yes.** There is assistance available for those who cannot afford a private attorney. The Puerto Rico Legal Services Corporation (Servicios Legales de Puerto Rico) provides free legal aid to low-income residents in areas like family law, housing, immigration, and consumer issues. In addition, the Public Defender's Office offers legal representation to individuals who are facing criminal charges and cannot afford to hire a lawyer.

Does your home country's embassy provide a list of local attorneys who speak English?

> **Yes.** Most embassies or consulates can provide a list of local attorneys, including those who speak English. Embassies often maintain a list of reputable lawyers in various fields to assist foreign nationals. You can typically access this list by contacting your embassy or consulate in Puerto Rico. *For more details, see Chapter 16.*

## Foreign Embassies in Puerto Rico

Are there foreign embassies/consulates in Puerto Rico?

**Yes**. Puerto Rico hosts many foreign consulates that provide services such as issuing passports, helping with legal issues, and offering assistance in emergencies.

Is there a website to locate embassies in Puerto Rico?

**Yes**. For a list of foreign consulates in Puerto Rico, you can refer to the U.S. Department of State's website, which provides a directory of foreign consulates in the U.S. territories, including Puerto Rico: **https://travel.state.gov/content/travel/en/consularnotification/ ConsularNotificationandAccess.html**. You can also visit the websites of individual foreign embassies or consulates for more specific information about services they offer and their contact details. *For more details, see Chapter 16.*

## Medical Facilities & Hospitals

Is there a number I can call for ambulance and fire emergencies?

In Puerto Rico, the **emergency number** to call for ambulance, fire, or police services is **911**, just like in the mainland United States.

If I am injured while on vacation in Puerto Rico, are there hospitals that are recommended for tourists?

**Yes**. If you are injured while on vacation in Puerto Rico, there are several hospitals that are equipped to handle emergencies and are recommended for tourists. Some of the well-known hospitals with good reputations for emergency care include **Hospital Pavia** (located in Santurce, San Juan), **Ashford Presbyterian Community Hospital** (in Condado, San Juan) and **Centro Médico de Puerto Rico** (in Río Piedras, San Juan). *For more details, see Chapter 17.*

## Driving in Puerto Rico

Which side of the road do I drive on?

In Puerto Rico, you drive on the **right-hand side** of the road, just like in the mainland United States.

Can I use my driver's license from my home country to drive in Puerto Rico?

**Yes.** You can use your driver's license from your home country to drive in Puerto Rico as a tourist, as long as it's in English or accompanied by an official translation. If you're staying for an extended period, you may need to apply for a Puerto Rican driver's license. However, it's a good idea to carry an International Driving Permit (IDP) alongside your foreign license if it's not in English.

How old do I need to be to rent a car?

The minimum age to rent a car in Puerto Rico is **21**. In certain cases, rental companies might have restrictions or higher rates for drivers under 25. Always check the specific terms of the rental agency you plan to use. *For more details, see Chapter 18.*

## Nude Beaches & Clothing-Optional Resorts

Is public nudity legal on the beaches?

**No.** Public nudity is generally not legal on Puerto Rico's beaches. While topless sunbathing is accepted in some areas, complete nudity is prohibited by public decency laws. Some private resorts may allow nudity, but it's best to check local rules or resort policies. *For more details, see Chapter 19.*

## Tourist Taxation

Is there room tax in Puerto Rico?

**Yes.** There is a room tax in Puerto Rico. The tax rate varies depending on the location and type of accommodation but generally ranges from **7 to 9 percent** for hotel rooms. Additionally, there may be other local taxes or resort fees applied, depending on the property.

Is there any fee associated with leaving Puerto Rico?

**No.** There is no departure tax for travelers leaving the island. However, any fees related to flights, such as baggage fees or airline taxes, would depend on the airline and are not specific to leaving Puerto Rico. *For more details, see Chapter 22.*

## Long-Term Stays

Do I need to return to my home country to apply for a work permit in Puerto Rico?

As an American citizen, you **do not** need to return to your home country to apply for a work permit in Puerto Rico. Since Puerto Rico is a U.S. territory, U.S. citizens can live and work there without requiring a separate work permit or visa. You would follow the same employment laws as you would on the mainland U.S. If you are not a U.S. citizen and want to work in Puerto Rico, you will need to obtain a work visa from a U.S. consulate or embassy.

As an American, how long can I stay in Puerto Rico without a visa?

As an American citizen, you can stay **indefinitely** in Puerto Rico without a visa. There are no time limits on your stay, as Puerto Rico is part of the United States. However, if you're planning to stay for an extended period and work, you may need to follow local employment regulations, such as getting a job and paying taxes in Puerto Rico. *For more details, see Chapter 23.*

## In the Event of Death

What documents would an embassy need regarding the death of a tourist?

If a tourist dies in Puerto Rico, the embassy will need the death certificate, identification (like a passport), and possibly an autopsy report if the cause of death is unclear. They will also require a notification of death from local authorities, travel and insurance details for repatriation, and consent forms for embalming or cremation. The embassy can assist with legal and logistical steps, including repatriation and funeral arrangements. *For more details, see Chapter 25.*

# EMERGENCY/IMPORTANT CONTACT NUMBERS IN PUERTO RICO

 Please consider putting some of these numbers in your phone prior to traveling to Puerto Rico.

## Helplines & Agencies:

- **Emergency Services:** 911
- **Police:** 787-343-2020
- **Ambulance:** 787-343-2222
- **Civil Defense:** 787-724-0124
- **Fire Department:** 787-343-2330
- **F.B.I:** 787-754-6000
- **U.S. Coast Guard:** 787-729-6770

## Other Important Numbers:

- **Abuse of Minors:** 787-749-1333
- **American Red Cross Blood Bank:** 787-759-7979
- **Federal Marshals:** 787-766-6000

- **Federal Emergency Management Agency (FEMA):** 787-729-7637
- **Humane Society of Puerto Rico:** 787-720-9398
- **Tourist Information:** 787-722-1709

## Legal Assistance:

- **Puerto Rico Bar Association:** +1 (787) -721-3358
- **Legal Aid (Servicios Legales de Puerto Rico):** +1 (787)- 728-8686

# USEFUL SPANISH PHRASES

## GREETINGS

**HI/HELLO** – Hola

**GOOD MORNING** – Buenos días

**GOOD AFTERNOON** – Buenas tardes

**GOOD NIGHT** – Buenas noches

**GOODBYE** – Adiós

## MAGIC WORDS

**PLEASE** – Por favor

**THANK YOU** – Gracias

**YOU'RE WELCOME** – De nada

**CHEERS!** – ¡Salud!

**EXCUSE ME** – Perdón/disculpe

## GETTING AROUND

**WHERE IS THE BATHROOM?** – ¿Dónde está el baño?

**WHAT TIME IS IT?** – ¿Qué hora es?

**HOW DO I GET TO…?** – ¿Cómo llego a…?

WHERE DOES THIS TRAIN/BUS GO? – ¿A dónde va este tren/autobús?

RESTAURANT – Restaurante

HOW MUCH DOES THIS COST? – ¿Cuánto cuesta esto?

TRAIN/METRO STATION – Estación de tren/metro

## COMMUNICATION

DO YOU SPEAK ENGLISH? – ¿Habla inglés?

I DO NOT UNDERSTAND – No entiendo

I DON'T SPEAK SPANISH – No hablo español

I DON'T KNOW – No sé

## EMERGENCY

HELP! – ¡Ayuda!

CALL AN AMBULANCE! – ¡Llame una ambulancia!

I NEED A DOCTOR – Necesito un doctor

POLICE – Policía

I'M LOST – Estoy perdido/a

IT'S AN EMERGENCY – Es una emergencia

# GLOSSARY

**ACQUITTAL**: A jury verdict that a criminal defendant is not guilty, or the finding of a judge that the evidence cannot support a conviction.

**ADVERSARY PROCEEDING**: A lawsuit arising from a controversy that begins with filing a complaint.

**AFFIDAVIT**: A written statement made under oath.

**APPEAL**: A request made after a trial court has decided against one party in which the losing party asks a higher court to review the decision for legal error.

**ARRAIGNMENT**: A proceeding in which a criminal defendant is brought to court, told of the charges, and asked to plead guilty or not guilty.

**BAIL**: The temporary release of a person from jail when awaiting trial, on condition that a sum of money be lodged or deposited to guarantee an appearance in court.

**BARRISTER**: A lawyer admitted to plead at the Bar and who may try cases in superior court.

**BURDEN OF PROOF**: The duty to prove disputed facts.

**CAUSE OF ACTION**: A legal claim in a civil action.

**COMPLAINT**: A written statement that begins a civil lawsuit in which the plaintiff details the claims.

**CONTRACT:** An agreement between two or more persons to do something or to not do something.

**CONVICTION:** A judgment of guilt against a person charged with a crime.

**CUSTOMS DUTY:** A tariff or tax imposed on goods when transported across international borders.

**COURT LIAISON:** A person that coordinates with attorneys to perform administrative duties, such as scheduling witnesses, sharing information with law enforcement, and overseeing the reporting of cases to foreign embassies when applicable.

**DAMAGES:** Money that a defendant pays to a plaintiff in a civil case if the plaintiff wins.

**DEFENDANT:** 1) The individual against whom a civil claim is filed; 2) The individual against whom a criminal claim is filed.

**FELONY:** A serious crime, punishable by more than one year in prison.

**MAGISTRATE:** A judicial officer of a district court, who conducts initial proceedings in criminal cases, decides criminal misdemeanor cases, conducts many pretrial civil and criminal matters on behalf of district judges, and decides civil cases with the consent of the parties.

**MISDEMEANOR:** An offense punishable by one year or less in jail.

**PLAINTIFF:** A person or business that files a formal complaint with the court.

**PLEA:** In a criminal case, the answer of "guilty," "not guilty," or "no contest" in response to a criminal charge.

**SOLICITOR:** A lawyer who advises clients, represents them in lower court, and prepares cases for barristers to try in higher courts.

**SOVEREIGN IMMUNITY**: A legal doctrine by which the sovereign or the state (i.e. government) cannot commit a legal wrong and thus, it is immune from criminal and civil liability and cannot be sued.

**STATUTE**: A written law passed by a legislative body.

**STATUTE OF LIMITATIONS**: A statute prescribing a period of limitation to bring certain types of legal actions. If the action is not brought within that time, the person or entity (in a criminal context) is permanently barred from suing in court.

**SUBPOENA**: A command, issued under court authority, for a witness to appear and to give testimony.

**TESTIMONY**: Evidence presented orally by witnesses.

**VERDICT**: The decision of a judge or jury in a case.

**WARRANT**: Court authorization to conduct a search or to make an arrest.

# ACKNOWLEDGMENTS

This book series would never have seen the light of day without the able assistance of the following people:

**Kathy Adams**, my paralegal for over 22 years, who is the "Best" I've ever worked with during my entire legal career because of her amazing work ethic, organizational skills, and her ability to think outside of the box in unique and creative ways;

**Ally Knez-Siddique**, a professional writer, and one of my paralegals, whose eye for detail, according to her, is both a blessing and a curse;

**Gino Ibanez**, my former law clerk, whose exceptional research skills helped move this book series along in its early stages;

**Rosa Diaz Graham**, my legal assistant who helped with research and word processing at the very beginning of this project;

**Shelia Martin**, one of my former paralegals, worked diligently on this series of books, even after taking on another job. Her organizational skills are reflected throughout;

**Mindy Scarlett**, my marketing and publishing "Guru"! Her creativity and vision have no boundaries!

# ABOUT THE AUTHOR

**Michael L. Moore** practices in Orlando, Florida, the city where he spent his formative years. He credits the trauma of having his brother murdered when he was only 10 years old, as the catalyst that drew him into the practice of law.

Moore attended Florida State University, where he was a member of the FSU debate team. Upon graduating, he was awarded a full scholarship to attend the University of Tennessee College of Law, where he was elected President of the Student Bar Association. He further honed his advocacy and public speaking skills by participating in 'moot court' competitions.

After clerking at the Tennessee Attorney General's office while in law school, Moore moved back to Orlando, Florida, to work at the State Attorney's Office as a prosecutor, and where he was fortunate enough to meet the young lady that would eventually become his wife. Moore moved on to working for private law firms, both local and national, and eventually established his own law firm in 1999. He continues to make Orlando his home base.

It was the murder of a close friend and client in Jamaica that caused Moore to realize that books on laws in other countries were few and far between, and he was inspired to create Law of the Land Publishing. Moore launched Law of the Land Publishing to provide a series of guide-books and a membership site for tourists and business travelers to stay up to date on the laws in each country they travel to, as well as having access to assistance if they run into legal issues.

"My vision is to educate people on what their legal rights are, and how they can access legal assistance, no matter where they have to travel to in the world," said Moore. "As Americans, we have a right to due process, but in some countries, you don't even have the right to access a square meal when incarcerated. My goal is to provide the information needed to stay out of trouble, as well as having access to assistance if trouble finds you."

.

www.ingramcontent.com/pod-product-compliance
Lightning Source LLC
Chambersburg PA
CBHW070912120626
46546CB00001B/229